TO. - MISS. SARAWAR -

FROM - ABG LINN. KMS -

PH: 09 312 88 546 -

BURMA.

20. P - 2019 -

D1178484

Up Close

Two Decades of Close Encounters with Aung San Suu Kyi

By Moe Linn (aka Pho Lay)

Translation
Khin Aung, Thaung Nyunt,
Ko Ko, Wai Linn

Proof Editor
Wade Guyitt

MCM BOOKS PUBLISHING
Myanmar Consolidated Media Ltd.
No. 379/383, Bo Aung Kyaw Street, Kyauktada Township, Yangon, Myanmar.
Phone: (01 392928)

Up Close

Two Decades of Close Encounters with Aung San Suu Kyi

By Moe Linn (aka Pho Lay)

Translated by MCM Translation

MCM MCM Books

© 2013 This book is produced by MCM Books, a wholly owned entity of
Myanmar Consolidated Media Ltd.
© 2013 MCM Company Limited,. 379-383 Bo Aung Kyaw Street,
Kyaukatada T/S, Yangon. Republic of The Union of Myanmar.
Telephone: +95 1 392 928 Facsimile + 951 254 158
email: administration@myanmartimes.com.mm
website: www.mmtimes.com
©2013 The title 'Up Close' Two Decades of Close Encounters with Aung
San Suu Kyi and the photographs and content contained within may
not be reproduced in whole or in part without the written consent of the
Managing Director of Myanmar Consolidated Ltd.
® 2013 All rights reserved.
Cover Price: 4,000 Kyats (Paperback)
                6,000 Kyats (Hard cover bound)
Circulation: 2,000 copies
Publisher by Zin Yadanar Publishing House (04084)
Printed by MCM Commercial Printing,
licence provided by Pyi Aye Family Press, Media Licence number (10371)
Photography: International - Agence France Presse
In Myanmar: Provided by Myint Soe and The Myanmar Times
Cover & Layout: Tin Zaw Htway, The Myanmar Times
Typography: Cover: ITC Avant Garde Gothic, Goudy, Garamond,
Text: Palatino Linotype, Helvetica Medium

Moe Linn (aka Pho Lay)   CIP-895.84
Up Close
Two Decades of Close Encounters with Aung San Suu Kyi
164 pages, 14.6 cm x 22.25 cm
(1) Up Close
    Two Decades of Close Encounters with Aung San Suu Kyi
    978-99971-0-066-5

Daw Khin Yi

(1930 - 2002)

"As I am getting older, I worry that I cannot come and see you at the prison" said my mother. There are only two members in my family, my mother and myself but she never worrys about what I am doing. I pay obeisance to my mother with these articles.

Moe Linn

Foreword

The first and foremost one who suggested compiling these articles was Sayar Doctor Tin Myo Win [Douglas (aka Ko Tar)]. As I took my daily duty of sending meals and household things for Ama (Daw Aung San Suu Kyi) and Sayar Tin Myo Win made medical check-up for Ama every month and we had a talk in 2006 and Sayar Tin Myo Win urged me to record about Ahma. I replied him that I also have the same idea.

In the middle of 2011, I can sense more openness and I tried to write as a trial run in some journals but the Press Scrutiny and Registration Department was still existed at that time.

One of the friends Sayar Maung Thway Thit is working at The Myanmar Times and I made contact him through the photographer Ko Kaung Htet. Sayar Maung Thway Thit also supported me of saying, "You should write and make records" and introduced me to Sayar Ko Zaw Myint. Suggestions were made how to write to be in-line with Press Scrutiny policy by Sayar Maung Thway Thit and Ko Zaw Myint. Also Sayar Thiha Saw from Myanma Dana urged me that I should write as I am the one with many records.

The pen-name "Moe Linn" was given by Sayar Gyi Min Theinkha. Sometimes I write with my previous pen-name "(KMS) Ko Myint Soe". I have to admit that I am only a young writer. As I have passed those years; 26 years under one party dictatorship and 23 years under military rule, I would like to share my experiences to others and I happened to write these articles. Please understand and forgive me of weakness in writing style and presentations.

I would like to express great thanks to Ama Daw Aung San Suu Kyi who always says, "Be well-behaved", the patrons of NLD who always read my articles and support me, *Ba Ba* U Win Tin who always teach me how to write, Sayar Ko Zaw Myint, Sayar Maung Thway Thit and The Myanmar Times staffs, Sayar Thiha Saw and Open News Journal staffs, The Myanmar Times Book Publishing Editors and all the people supporting to publish this book.

With great thanks,

Moe Linn (Pho Lay)

Contents

The birthplace of U Naung Cho, Ama's father

It was an honest confession of Ama's (Daw Aung San Suu Kyi's) father that Natmauk was a countrified place. However, it is a town in which pride should be taken. We think so. Such an honour cannot be made, nor can it be bought with money. The town was neglected by those who wanted to be honoured undeservedly. No wonder that Natmauk has not developed, if a Nautmauk native himself could be nearly erased from history. Let me recall something I have heard about it.

Almost 40 years ago, when the Pyithu Hluttaw was first convened in 1974, the representative for Natmauk (and chairman of the township's party unit), Salaing Tha Sein (or Salaing Kyaw Sein; I'm not sure), put forward a proposal to repair and renovate the mausoleum there. He did not get a definite answer. He asked the same question in following years, still with no concrete results. Eventually we no longer saw him around. He had been replaced by another man. (If he is still alive, please give him my best regards and tell him I am still proud of him.)

Natmauk is in a semi-desert region which is not suitable for cultivation. After Israel developed a technique to transform desert into arable land, it shared this scientific technique with the world. Every year, Myanmar sends agricultural scientists to Israel to study these advanced techniques. I wonder what they do after coming back from Israel.

People used to complain, "If only Bogyoke were still alive!" Don't rely too much on a midwife. You must make your own effort to deliver.

Some people from Natmauk moved to where the grass was greener and settled in new places. They became conceited and looked down on their old townfolk, rather than helping them any way they could.

One Natmauk native became a national hero, and his daughter has become world famous. How nice it would be if there were many doctors, engineers and military officers born in Natmauk. In reality what we mostly see, in the restaurants of Yangon and Mandalay, is that almost half of the waiters come from Natmauk. Most of them are boys under 18. While it is uplifting to hear them saying they came from Natmauk, it is also a pitiful sight.

The honest nature of Anyathians (folks from Upper Myanmar) is lovely and admirable. Since the old days, there has been a long tradition of the young people of Anya moving to other places for better opportunities. Today, some who have enough money go to Singapore, Thailand or Malaysia. Some of them are being cheated. Some go to jade and jewel mines, but most under 20 come down to Yangon.

When we were young, the Thayettaw monastery was the place to take refuge for Anya people. There they made money selling tamarind juice, *montletsaung* and cold *shweyinaye* drinks. Women sold Anya products such as thanakha, *ponyegyi* (thick brown sauce made from horse gram), jaggery, plum toffee, bean-rice cake and pickled sesame oil cake *(hnan bat chin)*.

Young women from Upper Myanmar came down to Yangon to seek a livelihood there, but the number of people who trade in traditional Anya products became fewer and fewer. Now they trade in vegetables, human hair, old newspapers, used papers and bottles and cans. Making a living out of whatever they can find is to be respected.

If you take a bus from downtown Yangon to North Okkalapa, when you get to Bahan Street 3 you will be at the place where a group of young women wearing long-sleeved shirts and thick thanakha on their cheeks used to get on. They were dealers in human hair. They used to give the conductor K1000 notes for the bus fare instead of smaller notes because they wanted the change. They needed to have

General Aung San

small currency ready for when they went round door-to-door in the residential quarters to buy hair. The bus conductors would get irritated by their behavior but the Anya girls just didn't care. The simplicity on their faces was lovely.

Early in the morning, at about 5:30, Anya girls with thanakha on their cheeks still get on the bus, hauling up their big baskets of vegetables. They go to sell their vegetables in Kamayut, Kyimyindine, San-chaung, Ahlone, Lanmadaw and Latha townships. In the baskets are limes, coriander, ginger, carrots and all kinds of beans. They sell them near the bazaars. They stop at about 10am and collect up the rest to sell again at the evening markets.

In former times they lodged at monasteries. Now they collectively rent apartments and live there together. Don't look down on them. Indeed! They are apartment dwellers.

Anya girls have also taken the place of "bottle Indians" (ethnic Indians who make a living by buying used bottles from households). The girls walk down the streets of residential quarters shouting and buying used bottles, cans, papers and old newspapers. Where have the "bottle Indians" gone? They are still in the garbage business, but they no longer go around town. Now they rent a ground-floor apartment for about K100,000 and buy the garbage that the girls have collected in the streets to sell back to the recyclers at a higher price.

Most of the boys under 18 work in restaurants. Conditions for the boys who work in more well-known restaurants are not so bad, as they get both a salary and free food. The life of the boys working in smaller restaurants depends on the moral nature of the owners. Good-natured owners treat them kindly, providing them with food and shelter, but the unlucky ones, those who have to work for ruthless owners, have to work day and night like slaves.

If you name any restaurant in Yangon, at least one of the waiters or chefs is likely to be a native of Natmauk. The boys who are already working in Yangon call their relatives and friends from Natmauk to come work in Yangon too. Now the son of Natmauk is our national hero and his daughter has become a world-famous democracy icon. So the name of Natmauk shall live forever.

Don't think, though, that just because a native of our town has become well known we will get special privileges and our town will develop more than others. No! Don't expect that. We won't be favoured. We will be treated the same as all citizens of the Union of Myanmar. Take, for instance, the case of President U Thein Sein. He is a native of Pathein, but he is not building cement mills or heavy industries near his hometown. He would not use his power to force the cronies to do that.

Everybody is sympathetic about the lack of development in Natmauk. At the opening ceremony of a hospital for eye diseases at Dipinkara monastery in Natmauk, Thitagu Sayadaw himself said he felt unhappy for the people of Natmauk area. He said, "Just like Lord Buddha belongs to the whole world despite the fact that he is Nepalese, so Bogyoke Aung San belongs to the whole Union of Myanmar because he was an architect of Myanmar's independence. So I have come to open a hospital for eye diseases here in Natmauk which has been left behind in development."

Don't ask a Myanmar crony for help. Instead, ask someone like George Soros, who came here recently. His foundation, OSF (Open Society Foundation), gives assistance to needy people around the world. He has been helping Myanmar nationals for 20 years, including those of RFA (Radio Free Asia) and DVB (Democratic Voice of Burma). When he came here recently, he said he was going to invest in Myanmar. Just try asking him for help for Natmauk.

– Open News (Vol. 5, No. 5, November 2012)

Encounter in a dream

While assigned the duty of minding Daw Aung San Suu Kyi's house, one day I packed up some old magazines and lay down with them on the bed. The magazines were the July 1956 and July 1957 issues of *Myawaddy*. I was reading reminiscences of Bogyoke Aung San, who was being written about by his colleagues in memory of the 10th anniversary of Martyrs' Day. Soon I grew tired and fell asleep.

I was woken up by the ringing of the doorbell. When I peeped through the hole at the gate, I saw a slim old man in a black *taikpone* (Myanmar jacket). I looked up at his face and realised that he happened to be Ama's father. I immediately opened the gate and let him in.

"Are you the father of Daw Aung San Suu Kyi?"

"Yes, I am," he said.

"Please come in."

"Who are you?"

"I am the caretaker of the house. Ama assigned me to mind the house while she is away."

"Where has my daughter gone?"

"They took Ama to Insein jail in May."

"Alas!" he exclaimed.

"She came here to attend to her ailing mother, but her mother passed away and she has been placed under house arrest. She is being tortured physically and mentally. Now she has again been sent to Insein jail. If Aung San Lin were still alive, he too would have been subjected to all kinds of torture. Brothers and sisters have similar natures and share the same views."

"I didn't understand why they bear a grudge against my family. My children are working for the good of our people and our country. We have never done anything for our own interest. As my daughter is sacrificing her life for the country like I did, people love her. I think they are jealous of her popularity. It's quite natural that the ones who seek self-interest don't like the ones who sacrifice for others. Well! Who are you? Why are you all alone in the whole house?" he asked.

"Uncle! Let me bring a tea-pot for you. Please enjoy some green tea."

"Good, go and get it."

I went into the kitchen and brought back a tea-pot and cups on a tray.

"I am a volunteer. I am helping Ama's campaign for democracy in my own small way. Ama left two men to look after the house. One is me and the other is a son of Thakin Ohn Myint, one of your colleagues in your struggle for independence. He is now undergoing a medical checkup. So I am alone in the house now. They moved her to Insein jail because a foreigner came into the compound."

"She is an important prisoner under house arrest. Even the road is blocked. How on earth did a foreign stranger come into the compound?

**General Aung San
with his family**

General Aung San with his family

Is there no guard at all?'

"There are guards. The commander himself stays here. Sentries are posted all around the house."

"Didn't anybody see a foreigner come in?"

"No, U Gyi, nobody did."

"Nonsense! Impossible!"

"They accused her of receiving the foreigner and took her away for interrogation. So I was assigned the task of minding the house."

"By the way, let me ask you: why do you address me as 'U Gyi' while everyone else calls me 'Bogyoke'?"

"In your day, there was only one Bogyoke: that was you. Now, there are many Bogyokes. So I would have to call you by your full name to address you. 'U Gyi' is easier to call you by."

"While there are some people who have forgotten me, others still remember me. People acknowledge me as a national leader and the founding father of the Tatmadaw. I've done nothing for my family or for myself. There may be some who are jealous of that. When a writer who wanted to write a biography of me went to my colleagues who are now in power and tried to ask them some questions about their past experiences, they said, 'Why do you bother to write a biography of that man? He has already gone.' The biographer was heartbroken to hear that. Because they wanted to make use of him, however, they brought up the things I said, my policy, hopes and plans, and used them to cheat the people. I know if I were still alive in 1962 I would have been put in jail.

"You see what my daughter is suffering through. She has no grudge or spite against them. They should treat her like their own daughter. When she was barely more than 20 years old, they tried to see if she was interested in or active in politics. Then they tried to find fault with her, saying that she was wrongly still holding a diplomatic passport. My daughter explained that she had applied for a passport extension a long time ago and they had done nothing about it. One of the men remarked on her boldness in replying to the officials this way.

"Then she replied, 'When the time comes, the blood of my father speaks out.'

"I am really sorry to learn that they have harboured a grudge against my daughter. I can understand and forgive some of my contemporaries who became jealous of my popularity, but I cannot understand the way some of the present-day leaders are treating me and my daughter. It is questionable that they are treating us like this. The Tatmadaw has grown to its present stage only because Hla Myaing (Bo Yan Aung) and I ventured to leave the country for military assistance from abroad. Yet after 26 years of the Burmese Way to Socialism and 23 more years under a military dictatorship, the country has become one of the least-developed countries in the world."

"No, U Gyi! The country has developed. They have put the people from the huts into multi-storey apartments. They have transformed the farmland into industrial zones with factories and workshops on it.

"If so, where did all the farmers go?"

"With compensations given by the state, they can now do whatever they like."

"If the farmer has no land to till, what else can he do? If he has no way of earning a living, he will come out on the street and demonstrate.

It is quite natural. They should not need motivation from others to act according to the law. Is there no law for the farmers?"

"Yes, there is a law of 1963 which says that the farmer who tills the land must own it. I don't know if there was a law for them in the 2008 constitution because I did not turn out to vote for it."

"Why didn't you turn out to vote in the referendum?"

"I believed that when hundreds of thousands of people were dying in a natural disaster, holding a referendum was not so important. It should have been postponed until a later time."

"That's right. Did they postpone it?"

"No, they didn't. They didn't try to rescue the cyclone victims who were trapped in helpless conditions. One of them even remarked that the fish would eat up the dead bodies and clean the area. They gave priority to voting in the referendum and they held it nationwide."

"What the hell! Voting more important than saving human lives? Do they mean it? Well! That's why your country is going down this way."

So saying, U Gyi left for the gate.

"Please, U Gyi, don't go back yet."

Uttering that, I woke up and realised that I was only dreaming. While reading a 1957 issue of *Myawaddy* magazine I had fallen asleep and met with Ama's father.

I had this dream in July 2009. That was three years ago now. During that period, changes have been abrupt and fast.

The speeches of minister U Aung Min from a meeting with political parties on July 22, 2012, were published in journals. His words were frank and friendly. U Aung Min recounted how, when he met with Harvard professors, they suggested that Myanmar members of parliament and cabinet members needed capacity-building and democracy training. U Aung Min admitted he had not been annoyed by what the professors said, because they made the suggestions with real goodwill and good intentions.

When I read this in the journal I came to understand what U Gyi meant by "capacity building". Speaking about the seizure of farmland, U Gyi said that the complaints of the farmers would one day come up. What he said has since come true. The farmers are speaking out now about their loss and the plight they are in. His past words are being proven true in the present day.

– The Myanmar Times (Vol. 31, No. 602, December 2012)

Bi-Lat Pyan Than (aka Dora Than Aye), the vocalist the founding father of the Tatmadaw loved to listen to

I'm rowing a small boat

Peaceful and calm

Cool and clear, near the bank of the river

(I don't remember the words)

Waterfall in the midst of thick jungle

Quite romantic!

(I remember no more)

I remember lyrics from three of Dora Than Aye's songs. "Hay-Wun-Nan", "Mya Pan Khway" and "Hlay ka Lay" are the songs of hers I like best. I am happy to know that my most respected Bogyoke also liked her songs. I am a man who follows the cult of personality. Just as I like the father of the Tamadaw, so I also like every military person. Myat Htan (Col. Tin Maung), Yaung Ni (Capt. Tin Lay) and Min Ye Htun are among the writers I like best. Sergeant Nyunt Khin's song "Pan Thit Sar" won the hearts of young girls. Dammika Ba Than (Col.

Ba Than) and Yarmanya Ko Ko Naing (Brigadier Khin Ohn) are also talented soldier-writers.

It was by strange coincidence that Bogyoke Aung San's family, Dora Than Aye and I became intimate friends.

Ever since I was a 10-year-old boy, I have admired Bogyoke Aung San. I read everything I could get about him. I noted down quotations from his speeches and writings and collected pictures of Bogyoke and his family, with whom I became acquainted by reading the biography and articles of Tekkatho Nay Win (Bo Htun Hla), Bogyoke's secretary. When I was young, every year on July 19 I waited until 10:37 to listen to the sound of the sirens signalling the time of at which Bogyoke Aung San and his cabinet members were assassinated. Then the melancholic songs of May Hla Myaing and Ko Mya Gyi would be heard on the radio. When I was a schoolboy and played truant, I used to go to Shwedagon Pagoda, or to Martyrs' Mausoleum, where I would sit against the tomb of Bogyoke Aung San and read what had been written about him. It was a calm and peaceful experience. At that time everybody was allowed to go there freely.

In the olden days, I often took bus No. 42 and bus No. 12, and whenever the bus passed No. 54 University Avenue, I bowed my head no matter if I was sitting or standing. It became habitual for me. When a friend who was with me one day asked me why, I said nothing. I had my own reasons.

Because I have read and noted down much about Bogyoke's family, I know where his children are living and with whom. I have pictures of Daw Khin Kyi, Bogyoke's wife, laying a wreath alone at the tomb 40 years ago, and pictures of Ama laying a wreath at the mausoleum later on. When I told my friends long ago what I had learned – that Ko Ko Oo was living in the USA, or that Ama Suu was in England and Dora Than Aye was taking care of her – nobody was interested in them then. (Some even accused me of worshipping Aung San. Now they are saying I am a Daw Aung San Suu Kyi worshipper.)

In 1969 or 1970, I saw a photo in a newspaper. It was of Daw Aung San Suu Kyi holding Khin Lay Myint Oo, the granddaughter of U Thant, Secretary General of the UN, on her birthday, which was celebrated at U Thant's home. U Thant's daughter Daw Aye Aye Thant and Bi-Lat

Pyan Than were also in the photo. I kept that newspaper cutting with me. In 1995, when I was a cook at Daw Aung San Suu Kyi's home, I showed her and it took her by surprise.

"It was 20 or 30 years ago," she said. "I have the original photo of this and I'll give it to you." So saying, she went upstairs and brought it back and gave it to me as a souvenir. It was 6" by 8" in size. Sometimes at the house when we watched documentary and biography films Ama took time to explain them to us despite her busy schedule. It is because of her goodwill that she wants us to be knowledgeable about the past.

That year, in the first week of October, Ama paid homage to Thamaya Sayadaw. She decided to make herself vegetarian three days in advance before leaving for Thamanya. After returning from Thamanya, she ate only vegetables and I prepared vegetarian food for her. Ama also asked me if I could also cook food for Dora Than Aye and family who were paying a visit to Yangon.

I was delighted to hear that. "Isn't it wonderful?" I thought. "I am going to have a chance to serve the singer that I have liked since I was young." This famous pre-war singer had taken care of Bogyoke's family for so long, but I had never dreamed of seeing Bi-Lat Pyan Than in person. I promised to take on the responsibility of preparing meals for the coming visitors.

Dora and family arrived in the last week of October. Patricia Gore-Booth (or "PGB") was also with them. She was the wife of Sir Paul Gore-Booth, who was Britain's ambassador to Burma from 1953 to 1956, and about whom there was an article published in *Working People's Daily* (Vol. 29, No. 86, December 25, 1991). The Gore-Booth family were very friendly with Daw Khin Kyi. In November, 1954, the Gore-Booths gave nine-year-old Aung San Suu Kyi an album of the family of Queen Elizabeth II, which remains well kept after 60 years. Ambassador Gore-Booth was transferred to India at the end of his service in Myanmar and became the British ambassador to India instead. In 1960, the Myanmar government appointed Daw Khin Kyi as an ambassador of Myanmar to India (Myanmar's first-ever female ambassador). The Gore-Booths and Daw Khin Kyi's family were united again in New Delhi.

As Dora Than Aye was at that time working in India, at the UN, she and Aung San Suu Kyi became friendly. Ama then introduced Dora Than Aye to PGB and they became friendly too. When Dora left India for Algeria to serve in the UN there, Ama went with her to explore the region and learn more about it. Led by Ahmed Benbela, Algeria had been freed from being a French colony. Ama arrived just as Benbela was being ousted by Bumidien. Ama had a chance to witness the instability of post-colonial Algeria firsthand. When Ama left for England in 1964 to study at Oxford, PGB's family undertook the responsibility of looking after her education and well-being.

Around 1970, Daw Khin Kyi was working at UN headquarters in New York. Their family friend Frank Trager, professor of international relations at New York University, helped Ama attend postgraduate classes there. Ama lived with her mother in Manhattan. As NYU is rather far from Manhattan, it was a long, hard journey each day for Ama, who used to feel giddy after riding the bus for long distances.

While studying for her postgrad degree, Ama applied for a job at the UN. After hurdling past the usual formal tests and interviews, she got a job at UN headquarters. The post was "assistant secretary of the advising committee for administrative and financial affairs at the office of the UN Secretary General". While working at the UN, Ama took part in volunteer work for the health and social welfare of helpless elderly people.

PGB was known to be fond of *kinpungyin* soup and fried dry *nga-gyi*. So I prepared this meal especially for her. Dora Than Aye liked it as well. When I saw how kindly Dora took care of Ama, I wished Bogyoke could have seen it for himself. The singer he loved was now taking care of his daughter as if she were her own, and in return Ama called Dora "Aunty Daw Than Aye". PGB also looked after Ama very kindly.

One day, before Dora Than Aye left Myanmar on November 10, she said, "I'll take a picture of you to remember you by." She took my photograph in the kitchen. Then, on the morning of the day she left, she said, "Whenever I see you, you are always wearing a T-shirt with Suu Suu's picture on it. I have only got a brooch with a picture of Suu Suu. Accept it for remembrance." She gave me the brooch and then we exchanged addresses. Dora left at 7 o'clock that day.

Every year since then, Dora Than Aye sent me postcards with notes

Bi-lat Pyan Than aka **Dora Than Aye**

on them. Some years I received them and some years I didn't. The card
I received on December 1, 1999, was one of the last. It was the year
Michael (Ama's husband) passed away. She wrote in her letter that
she had travelled twice that year. She got tired easily because she had
grown older and was at that time nearing 90. She attended Michael's
funeral and held a prayer gathering on the day six months after his
death. For her to visit Myanmar again would depend on the availability
of visas. She wrote that she missed Ama and wanted to write to her
too, and she wrote about her wishes and dreams. She said how PGB
and she were taking care of Michael's burial together (PGB also sent
me photographs of Michael when he had received the honorary degree
awarded by Melbourne University on his wife's behalf). To read her
letters was to feel sorry for her. I wished that someday Dora and PGB
would be able to come back here again.

It was a busy year, maybe near the end of 2008, when Ni Ni (Thakin
Ohn Myint's son) said, "Hey! I heard your Kyee Kyee (Dora) passed
away, but I am not certain yet."

There was a pain deep in my heart. I didn't know who to ask to find

Gore-Booth
152 Rivermead Court
Ranelagh Gardens
London SW6 3SF

London May 22 1999

Dear Myint Soe,

I was delighted to get your nice card and kind greetings when Kim arrived back from Burma. Now Alexander is leaving on the 24th and will bring my best wishes and kind regards to you. It is wonderful that Daw Suu has been able to see both her sons again. We are all so very sad about Michael and miss his kindness and wisdom and affection every single day. I am glad Daw Suu has such faithful friends and supporters like you. We all pray for better things to come soon. I spoke to Nathan E yesterday & she sends her greetings too.

With my affection & thanks to you all

Patricia Gore Booth.

UDAIPUR
by Tim Scott Bolton
Sold in aid of
the children of
DR. GRAHAM'S HOMES,
Kalimpong, W. Bengal, India.

Letter from Patricia Gore Booth (wife of Sir Lord Gore Booth, Ex-British Ambassador to Myanmar) to author.

out more. I was acquainted with Dora thanks to Ama, so Ama would know all about it, but she was busy when I tried to talk to her. I read an old article by Tekkatho Sein Tin in *The Myanmar Post* titled "Thet Wai song sung by Bogyoke Aung San in London". Then I hit upon the idea that I should write about Dora Than Aye. I am the one who met with Dora Than Aye in person in Yangon. So I started writing this article to pay homage to the late Bilat Pyan Than, famous pre-war vocalist.

Waterfall in the midst of thick jungle

Quite romantic!

I have done meritorious deeds for you, Kyee Kyee. Now you say *sadu* from a higher layer of existence. I believe you'll take care of Ama from your higher noble existence.

(To Dr Tin Myo Win, who suggested that we, who lived near Ama, should record what should be recorded.)

– The Myanmar Times (Vol. 27, No. 536)

Bi-lat Pyan Than (with head scarf) and Daw Aung San Suu Kyi's family.

called you her "Foster Aunty", "Kyee Kyee". Daw Aung San Suu Kyi and her relatives always use Myanmar usage such as Phay Pyay, May May, Daw Gyee, Daw Lay, Kyee Kyee, Ma Ma, Ma Ma Tin Hla, Ma Ma Chaw, Ko Ko Aye, Ko Ko Oo, Ko Ko Lin, Ko Htwe, Cho Cho, Ko Ko Nyi, etc.

I still remember how, on a visit to Yangon in 1995, you and PGB attended Ama's speech to the crowd of supporters in front of her house. This was the last time you two were together. You passed away in 2008 and PGB passed away February 13, 2012, but how happy you both would have been, if you were still alive, to see Ama once again visiting Europe.

The president of Switzerland welcomed Ama at state level with full security. In Norway, the king and queen hosted a dinner for her and honoured her with her Nobel Peace Prize for 1991. Bono, of the pop band U2, took her on his private jet to Dublin. Maung Htein Lin, Ama's son, waited for his mother in Norway. Her 67th birthday party was held in Oxford. It is a pity that you and Michael were not there with Suu's family, Aunty. She received an honorary Doctorate of Law from

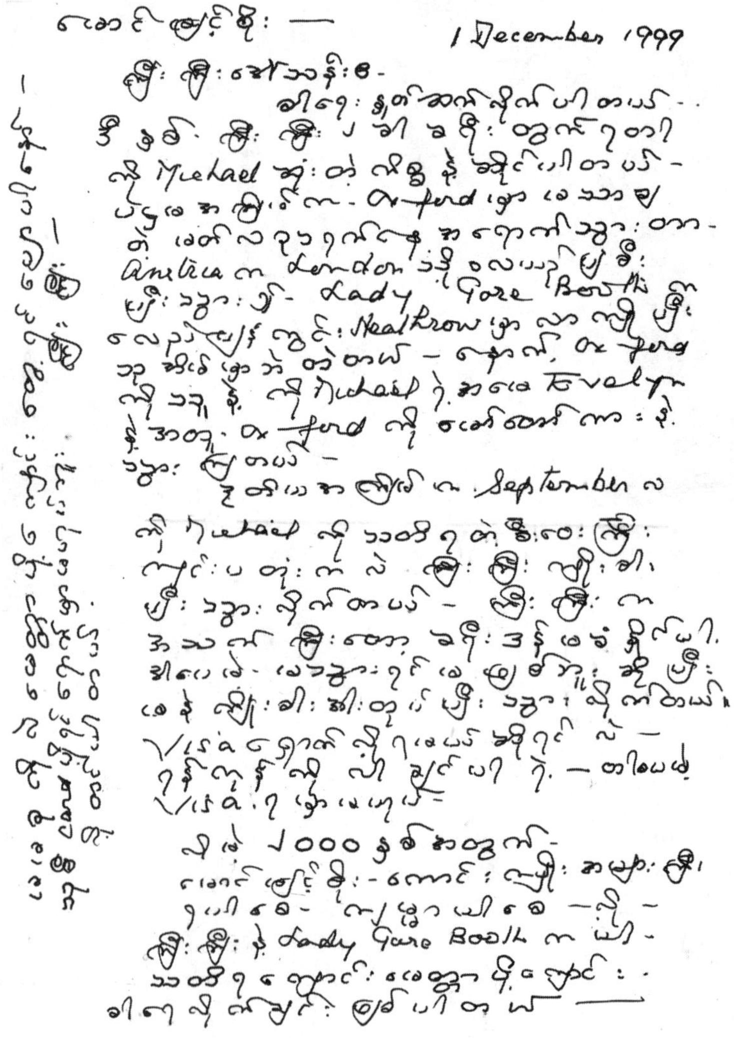

1 December 1999

Bi-lat Pyan Than's original hand-writing

Oxford. Prince Charles and Lady Camilla received Ama at the palace. Ama was welcomed by the prime minister at No. 10 Downing Street, where her father had signed an agreement with then-Prime Minister Atlee. Ama became the first woman, the first person from Asia and only the fifth person overall to be allowed to speak at a joint assembly of the Upper and Lower Houses in Westminster Hall in Central London.

Dear Kyee Kyee, I believe the three of you will take pride in Ama Suu from the next life.

– The Myanmar Times (Vol. 29, No. 576, 2012)

The Nehru and Aung San generations

When I started to take an interest in literature around 1964-65, I started to read biographies. Among the biographies I read were those of Bogyoke Aung San, Mahatma Gandhi, Jawaharlal Nehru, Indira Gandhi, John F. Kennedy and Che Guevara. I read the biographies of Bogyoke Aung San, Nehru and Indira Gandhi so many times that I felt like I was acquainted with the members of their families.

It is because of these books that I am familiar with names like Bogyoke Aung San, Daw Khin Kyi, Ko Ko Oo (Aung San Oo), Ko Ko Lin (the late Aung San Lin) and Ma Ma Suu (Aung San Suu Kyi). Likewise, other names to remember for me are Motilal Nehru, Jawaharlal Nehru, Pandit Nehru, Indira Gandhi, her husband Feroze Gandhi, son Rajiv Gandhi, daughter-in-law Sonia Gandhi, younger son Sanjay Gandhi, daughter-in-law Maneka Gandhi and grandchildren Rahul Gandhi and Priyanka Gandhi. I also read about the Kennedy family: Fitzgerald Kennedy, Rose Kennedy, John F. Kennedy, Robert Kennedy and Edward Kennedy. The three brothers were very popular at that time. After John F. Kennedy's death, his wife Jacqueline Kennedy, his son John F. Kennedy, Jr. and his daughter Caroline Kennedy were often seen in the world media.

Ama's father was known to be very friendly with Nehru. When Bogyoke stopped over in India en route to England in January 1947 to hold discussions with the British government, he was welcomed by Nehru and his daughter Indira. Nehru, who had studied in England and know what the London weather was like, gave Bogyoke a warm long coat to wear there, and had another tailored to his measurements overnight and given to him. When I read about this, I became very fond of Nehru and his family. When Daw Khin Kyi was appointed ambassador to India, Prime Minister Nehru and his daughter were very friendly toward her as the widow of the late Bogyoke Aung San. During her tenure as ambassador, he gave her a government mansion on Akbar Road in New Delhi, where Daw Suu attended a college.

By reading about Gandhi and Nehru I became conversant with Indian politics, the struggle of Gandhi and Nehru and the role of the Congress Party in India's independence struggle. I came to realise that the Nehru family and the Congress Party were inseparable.

The Congress Party was founded in the early 19th century under British rule. (I don't remember the exact date.) It has been a major political party since Motilal Nehru, Jawaharlal's father, and the legacy continues even to Rahul Gandhi and Priyanka Gandhi, Nehru's great-grandchildren, and to Sonia Gandhi, Nehru's granddaughter-in-law. (Later generations sometimes confuse Nehru's descendents with Mahatma Gandhi, as their surnames are Gandhi also. It started with Indira Gandhi, who married Feroze Gandhi to become Indira Gandhi. Mahatama Gandhi and Nehru were not related.)

Indira Gandhi was a key figure in the Nehru family. The book *Letters from a Father to his Daughter* was well known all over the world. Because of Nehru's book, Indira became known to the world. Kamala Nehru, Nehru's wife, was always in poor health, so she was not capable of taking part in political activities. All members of the Nehru family became well known but none of them was as famous as Indira Gandhi. The Nehru family legacy continues today because of her.

In her childhood, Indira was often left alone with servants at home while her father and grandparents were away taking part in demonstrations led by Gandhi-ji. She had to pass the time playing with toys. Her toys were British soldiers and she played at people rising up just like her father and grandparents were doing in real life.

When Indira came of age, she had no time to pay attention to education because she had to attend to her ailing mother who was undergoing treatment in Switzerland and England. She paid regular visits to her father and Mahatma Gandhi in prison, however, so she received their political legacy. She possessed the capacity to organise the unity of all the people of India.

The Nehru family is believed to be the only one in the whole world that has handed down a political legacy to four successive generations by democratic and not autocratic means. Nehru, Indira Gandhi, Rajiv Gandhi, Rahul Gandhi, Priyanka Gandhi and Sonia Gandhi have all been party leader of the Congress Party.

In my mind's eyes, I can still recall a photograph of Prime Minister Nehru, his daughter Indira Gandhi, Rajiv Gandhi and Sanjay Gandhi. Sanjay was driving a toy car. Maybe it was in Nehru's biography. I believed Rajiv and Sanjay would lead India someday. Sanjay turned out to be what I had expected but unfortunately his love of flying (he was a pilot) led to his untimely death when his private plane crashed.

Just as Daw Khin Kyi was friendly with Nehru and Indira Gandhi, Ama was also friendly with Indira Gandhi, Rajiv Gandhi and Sanjay Gandhi.

When Nehru died, his colleagues eyed Indira as his successor, except for Morarji Desai who underrated her and scorned the Nehru family. The Congress Party chose Lal Bahadur Shastri instead of Morarji Desai for prime minister. Before long, when Bahadur Shastri passed away, Morarji Desai tried to take hold of the Congress Party with his supporters, but the veteran party members, who backed the Nehru family, organised the Congress (I) Party which elected Indira Gandhi. Indira was elected prime minister (the second Nehru generation to be so) and Desai's group came to an end.

Sanjay, Indira's younger son, was interested in politics. He was active in the Congress Party and was believed to be his mother's political heir. After his death, Indira Gandhi brought her elder son, Rajiv – who preferred a peaceful, quiet life – into politics in Sanjay's place. Maneka Gandhi, Sanjay's widow and Indira's daughter-in-law, was displeased with her mother-in-law and decided to defect from Congress (I) to join the opposition. Eventually she withdrew from politics.

When Indira was killed by her own bodyguard, who bore a grudge against her for a raid on a Sikh temple by Indian troops, Rajiv led the Congress Party and became prime minister of India (making him the third generation of the Nehru family to hold this position).

Rajiv Gandhi was also killed, by a Tamil Tiger suicide bomber. I was really sad to see Sonia Gandhi, her son Rahul Gandhi and her daughter Priyanka Gandhi at Rajiv's funeral. The faces of Rahul and Priyanka reminded me of Indira Gandhi. They seemed to take after their grandmother. Priyanka especially looks like Indira. They are Nehru's fourth generation. After the death of Rajiv Gandhi, the Congress Party started to lose power, though it survived as an opposition party for many years. Sonia has brought up her son and daughter to be active young members of the Congress Party. Priyanka, now married, was seen in a demonstration, a sign, I believe, that Nehru's fourth generation will come up soon. Rahul is now a member of parliament and he too is expected to be a leader of India. When Jawaharlal Nehru and his father Motilal Nehru were arrested for taking part in the peaceful demonstrations of Mahatma Gandhi, Motilal's wife took part in the demonstrations on behalf of her husband and son. Now Rahul and Priyanka are following in the footsteps of their great-grandparents.

Sonia has been able to rebuild the Congress Party to win again in elections. She was the chairperson of the party so she had to be prime minister but she chose to let Manmohan Singh take the post instead. She had lived closely with her mother-in-law Indira Gandhi, so she had learned the political lessons of India along with her husband Rajiv.

There is no discrimination against members of the Nehru family who get married to different races and religions. Sonia met Rajiv at Oxford University and became an Indian citizen after following Rajiv to India. She dresses like an Indian woman and the people adore her. She speaks Hindustani and lives in the Hindu tradition. Priyanka is known to have married a man of a different race and religion. Priyanka Gandhi is the latest of Nehru's descendents. Sanjay and Maneka had a child, but little is known about him, probably due to Maneka's attitude toward her mother-in-law, Indira Gandhi. At the moment the people of India are expecting much from Rahul Gandhi, the fourth generation of the Nehru family, because Nehru is the heart and soul of India just as Bogyoke Aung San is that of Myanmar.

– The Myanmar Times (Vol. 27, No. 537, 2011)

References:
1. Indira Gandhi (by Soe Myaing)
2. Nehru (Thamameitta Publishing)

Thakhin Ohn Myint, comrade of
Thakhin Aung San

It has been two years now since *Aba* (Grandpa) Thakhin Ohn Myint passed away, but he is still alive in my mind. I would like to recount my reminiscences of Thakhin Ohn Myint. Though he was a historic figure, people who didn't know him would not think highly of him. He had his own style. When I first saw him, I thought he was an old Chinese man. He was wearing blue jeans, walking shoes and a cap, and had a Shan-style bag slung over his shoulder.

When I asked, I was told that this old man was Thakhin Ohn Myint, a comrade of Bogyoke Aung San's, and that Ama herself grew up under his care. I met him in Ama's compound in 1989. He was modest, free and entirely without pomposity. I became friendly with him only in 1995. I like reading so when I asked about his experiences in historic events he told me. I am in the habit of collecting what I am interested in. So I shared my collected materials with him whenever he wanted. I had a copy of a letter written by Ama to the State Council on August 15, 1988. It was called "Advice to the State Council". I had kept it for so long, but when Aba Ohn Myint asked me to give it to him, I had to oblige him. I also had a copy of an old journal which carried a picture of

Ama making her first speech at Rangoon General Hospital on August 23, 1988. At her side were Maung Thaw Ka and movie star Khin Thida Tun. This also was transferred to Aba Thakhin Ohn Myint, but I have to confess that I didn't want to, because these were among the rare parts of my collection.

Thakhin Ohn Myint was born to U Moe Kaung and Daw Aye Tin on April 28, 1918, at Letpadaung. He started his political activity in 1933 while in high school in Letpadaung, distributing slogans and pamphlets against imperialism and colonialism. His schoolteacher was Journal-Kyaw U Chit Maung. Having passed his matriculation examinations, in spite of his eligibility for medical science he decided to enter the media world in Yangon.

In 1936 he wrote an article titled "Not Fast and Hard, but Slow and Soft, Myanmar" in the *Myanmar Alin* newspaper. He continued to write articles and novels by such pen-names as Saenhityathi Pyone and Myint Ohn. He lived with *Journal Kyaw* U Chit Maung at Hnin-pan street in Ye Kyaw quarter, Yangon.

He attended the second All-Burma Students' Congress, which convened in Mandalay in 1937, and also the third All-Burma Students' Congress, which was held in Pathein in 1938. In 1938 he was the editor of *Toetetye* newspaper and assumed the *Thakhin* prefix as part of his name. He was the joint publisher of The *Journal Kyaw* newspaper and wrote many articles on current-day politics in Burma.

In January 1939, because of an article written by him under the pen-name of Semi-khwet, the Colonial government set bail for *Toetetye* newspaper.

He was one of the six members of Doebama-Aseayone invited by the All India Congress Party to attend the Runger Conference in March 1940, together with Thakhin Aung San and Thakhin Than Tun.

He was active in the anti-fascist movement from 1942 to 1945. From 1951 to 1964, he published political books with the publishing house Kyaw Lin Sar Pay.

In 1958, at the time of the caretaker government, he was arrested under Article 5 and sent to Coco Island. In 1989, he was again sentenced to five years in prison under Article 5(j). In November 1996, he was

Thakhin Ohn Myint

detained for 20 days in connection with student demonstrations. In January 1998, he was sentenced to seven years in prison for assisting Ko Aung Tun in writing a history of the Students' Union.

He was a politician of such honour, but as far as I know he was not involved in party politics. He only enjoyed associating with political activists. At Ama's request, though, he did take part in the NLD's social aid group.

Let me tell you about the emergence of the social aid group. In October 1995, Ama went to pay homage to the Thamanya Sayadaw. On the way back, Ama asked me about my experiences in prison. I told her that, after being released, I visited the families of those in prison on Mondays and Saturdays to give whatever aid I could give. (At that time some of my colleagues were still in prison and there were also newcomers whose families had no knowledge of prison life. This was during the years 1991-1993.)

Not long after her return from Thamanya, Ama started organising social aid groups with Aba Thakhin Ohn Myint, Ko Htein (U Win

Htein, hluttaw member for Meiktila), E-bar aka Tin Hlaing, Ni Ni Wai (Tamwe) and Ko Saw Hlaing (Dagon township) as members. They made a list of prisoners' families and gave assistance to them.

The present social aid group of NLD was based on this small group born in Ama's compound. Thakhin Ohn Myint led the group until the day he died. He was always seen at every social occasion for families of prisoners and politicians. Thakhin Thein Maung (Wakhema) was his usual partner. He always attended the annual occasions of Ludu Daw Amar and Sayagyi Dagon Taryar. Because of his old age, his family members worried whenever he went outside, but he never heeded their worries and always did what he wanted. That is how he was.

Thakhin Ohn Myint led an interesting life. After the death of his wife, he was left with four children. He lived with one son and one daughter and the other son and daughter lived abroad. So he lived carefree. Because he was getting old but was still active in politics, his children worried about his safety. Their worry was quite sensible, because he was taken away and imprisoned time after time, but he always acted in accordance with his convictions.

One thing I liked about Aba Ohn Myint (maybe because it is somewhat similar with me) was that he didn't care much about what he wore. The clothes you are wearing are only superficial. What matters most is the soul underneath. I like this philosophy. I hate the man who shows off like an important person, always wearing a collarless white shirt and a *taikpone*.

Aba Thakhin Ohn Myint never pretended. He practised politics while wearing blue jeans, a T-shirt and walking shoes. He was not influenced by anyone but *Ama*. When *Ama* asked him to wear a reddish-brown pinni *taikpone* and a cotton longyi, he dared not refuse. He regarded *Ama* as his own daughter and didn't want to disappoint her. Because of this, you would always see Aba wearing national costume at occasions sponsored by Ama. Apart from these occasions, however, he was always seen wearing jeans and walking shoes.

I met Aba almost every day during the years while *Ama* was in house arrest because *Ama* had assigned Aba's son Ko Htay Aung and me to bring daily meals to her from Aba's house. If Ko Htay Aung was busy, I took over the duty and vice versa.

Ko Htay Aung is a solitary kind of person. Unlike his father he always lives alone. Father and son love each other very much, but when friends asked Aba if his son was feeling well, he would reply that he had died already. Likewise, when someone asked Ko Htay Aung if his father was feeling well, he used to reply, "You'd better go and ask him."

Aba thought that his son was not behaving himself. His son thought his father should take rest and live quietly because he was getting old. So they lived standoffishly. They never talked to one another directly. Instead, messages were relayed through a middleman. For instance, if Ko Htay Aung wanted to tell his father something, he would ask me to send the message to his father, and vice versa. They loved each other that much.

Anyway, Aba loved his son whom he called by the name Ni Ni. He was annoyed only because he thought his son was not well behaved. Ko Htay Aung is good-natured but he is never sweet and is clever in talking, so I squabbled with him frequently.

Just think about it. There were only three people in Aba's family. Only Aba thought along the same lines as me. When I came to his

Thakhin Ohn Myint

house, Aba used to enquire about *Ama* and what she wanted. His son didn't want me to talk about *Ama*, but Thakhin Ohn Myint was no other person, so I had to tell him. Thakhin Ohn Myint regarded *Ama* as his own daughter, but Aba also understood his son very well and never asked me anything in front of him. Sometimes he seemed to want to eat the same food as *Ama* had asked me to buy for her. So Aba asked me buy the same food for him. Then Ko Htay Aung exploded and told his father he would buy it for him and that he should not have asked me. Ko Htay Aung didn't want his father to get involved in serving *Ama* and give me additional duty.

I knew the offbeat food *Ama* used to have a taste for, so when I bought such food, Aba would ask me to buy some more for him. I happily did what he asked me to, but then his son would blame me for pampering his father, so we would get into a squabble again.

In 2008, while on a train journey to the birthday party of Sayagyi Dagon Taryar, Aba got ill. Ni Ni followed him and took him back from Nyaunglebin. After that, his health deteriorated and he didn't attend any more events and had to stay at home. Sometimes he would take a look at the things I bought for *Ama* and asked what was what. If his son appeared, he suddenly turned, went still and pretended not to have asked anything. His pitiable behaviour never went out of my mind.

On May 13, 2009, *Ama* called Ni Ni and me and assigned us the task of taking care of the house. I cooked rice but the curry and dishes for the two of us were brought from Aba's house. Whenever I went to get the dish, Aba would ask about his son. I said that Ni Ni was good now, not like before. I also had to tell him about *Ama* whenever Aba asked.

After *Ama* came back home on August 11, 2009, I was allowed to cook for her for a week. *Ama* asked me to tell Aba that he would be the first to see her once she was allowed to see visitors. Aba was happy to hear that. At the end of a week, we were told that food had to be sent in from outside as before. With *Ama*'s permission, I was given the chance to prepare and send the daily meals to her. While waiting for the day when he would get permission to see *Ama*, Aba Thakhin Ohn Myint passed away on the morning of September 17, 2010, just two months before *Ama*'s release from house arrest. I felt sorry for Aba, who had not had a chance to see *Ama* – whom he had loved as his own

From Left to Right- Taw Phayar Galay, Cartoon U Pe Thein, Parachute U Ohn Maung, Sayar Gyi Taik Soe, Thakhin Ohn Myint, Writer Tin Thein Maung, Architect U Kyaw Min and wife of Taw Phayar Galay-Daw Khin May. (All deceased except Daw Khin May)

daughter – free from all chains. Likewise, how happy he would be, if he could see his son Ni Ni now doing well and driving a Harrier car!

(In memory of Thakhin Ohn Myint, who died on September 17, 2010)

– The Myanmar Times (Vol. 30, No. 594, 2012)

Thamee Shwewar, Martyrs' Day
is drawing near

Martyrs' Day is coming again. Do you still remember the day? Don't confuse Arzarni Day with the birthday of pop singer R. Zar Ni. They are quite different.

Martyrs' Day is a day of mourning, the anniversary of the day on which Bogyoke Aung San and his colleagues were assassinated just before the country's independence. Bogyoke Aung San was many things: a student leader, the politician Thakhin Aung San, the revolutionary Bo Tay Za, the founder of Tatmadaw Bogyoke Aung San, the father of independence and our national leader. So the day of his untimely death was designated Martyrs' Day, one of the gazetted holidays of Myanmar.

On July 19, 1947, while Bogyoke Aung San and his cabinet members were holding a meeting, a group of assassins came in and killed all of them. Bogyoke Aung San was the main target, but all the fallen leaders were honoured on the same level and buried at a place just north of Shwedagon Pagoda named Martyrs' Mausoleum. It was a day of disaster for the nation and a setback on a national scale.

Why don't some want to accept these facts? Why do they want to forget it and remove it from history? Can true history be distorted and dismissed? If you want to be revered and respected, you just have to sacrifice your own interest for the country as they did. Instead, some seem to have been trying to be included in the list of the world's most notorious 200.

Honour cannot be demanded or commanded, nor can it be invented. It must be acknowledged and gained deservedly. Such names as national leader, architect of independence, revolutionary leader are given by the people to those who are deserving of such titles. If you try to take them forcefully, you can only get submission to your authority. It will be difficult to win the people's hearts. You should try to gain honour in ways which are acceptable to the world. We should take pride in the fact that our President U Thein Sein was included in the list of 100 world leaders notable for their courage and vision. We honour leaders like Jose Rizal Juliet Phuchit, Che Guevera, Nguyen Van Tri etc. We are disgusted by leaders like Hitler, Mussolini, Stalin, Saddam Hussein, Hosni Mubarak, Charles Taylor, Milosevic, Maladics, Hugo Chavez, Amadinejad and Kim Jong-Un. Reformers like Mikhail Gorbachev are always sure to emerge.

When we were young, seminars and talks about Martyrs' Day were held one week in advance. Pamphlets about Martyrs' Day were distributed legally. The ministry itself issued these papers. On Martyrs' Day, students would go around by bus to places like the Bogyoke museum and Bogyoke's statue at Kandawgyi and pay respect to Bogyoke. Factories and mills, as well as the Burma Broadcasting Service (BBS), blared their sirens precisely at 10:37am, the time the martyrs were gunned down by the wicked assassins. Everybody everywhere stood still and bowed down to the fallen leaders. The people on the street stopped to pay respect. After that, BBS played songs honouring the martyrs, such as those of vocalist May Hla Myaing. At 8:15pm, after the news, the speeches of Bogyoke Aung San were aired.

In the days gone by, the Martyrs' Day wreath-laying ceremony was held at state level and attended by the head of state himself. Then, in the era of Burma's socialist program, it was held at the ministerial level and attended by the Minister of Culture. Nowadays, it is being held at city level, attended by the mayor only. It looks like they are doing it unavoidably and perfunctorily.

In olden days, every year on Martyrs' Day, *sanghas* (monks), were offered *soon* (a meal) at city hall, and they shared the merit with the fallen leaders. In the papers there were pictures of Daw Khin Kyi pouring water and sharing merit with her late husband U Aung San and his comrades. People from all walks of life marched in procession to Arzarni Hill to salute the *arzarnis* (martyrs), namely Dee-Doke U Ba Cho (minister), Thakhin Mya (minister), U Ba Win (minister), Maing Pun Saw Bwa Gyi Sao San Tun (minister), Bogyoke Aung San, Mann Ba Khaing (minister), U Razak (minister), U Ohn Mg (secretary) and Ko Htwe (bodyguard).

The old mausoleum was built of timber in the traditional Myanmar architectural style. The tombs were labelled with the names and photographs of each leader so it was easy to know which tomb was whose. Now there is a new mausoleum, with a new design. The public are not allowed to come near them. It is not possible to know where each tomb is. Nowadays, the only tomb of an international standard is that of writer Thakhin Ko Daw Hmaing. Someday that will also change.

The story of the emergence of the new mausoleum is like this. On October 9, 1983, General Chun Doo-Hwan, who took over power in South Korea as president, paid an official visit to Yangon. One of his scheduled events was the laying of a wreath at Martyrs' Mausoleum. In former days, international leaders who paid an official visit to Myanmar used to lay wreaths at Martyrs' Mausoleum. It was an international practice. In every country there are national heroes or fathers of freedom who are honoured and respected by the whole country. For example, in India, foreign leaders visit and lay wreaths at the tomb of Mahatma Gandhi, and in Vietnam, wreaths are laid at the tomb of Ho Chi Minh. Similarly, foreign leaders lay wreaths at Martyrs' Mausoleum when they come to Myanmar.

On learning about the South Korean president laying a wreath at the mausoleum, the government of North Korea sent spies to Myanmar more than one month ahead of Chun Doo-Hwan's arrival. Disguised as sailors, they disembarked from a cargo ship which was loading and unloading at the port of Yangon. They lodged at a house in Ahlone township which had been rented in advance by the North Korean embassy. The spies studied the environment around the mausoleum for more than a month. Two days before President Chun's arrival, the spies left the house in Ahlone and slept in the bushes opposite the western entrance of Shwedagon Pagoda on the other side of U Wisara Road (there used to be bushes and jungle there, as there was no People's Park yet). After dark they went up to the mausoleum and installed bombs on the beams and ceiling. Nobody noticed their activity.

President Chun was scheduled to lay the wreath at 10am on October 9. He was staying at Green Lake State Guest House on University Avenue. His motorcade came from Hledan to the Hanthawaddy roundabout, then along U Wisara Road to Arzani Hill. The North Korean spies waited at the junctions and signaled. When the motorcade came along University Avenue around 9 o'clock, the spies thought President Chun was in it and relayed the message. In fact, it was an advance party comprising foreign ministers and deputy ministers. Their group arrived at the mausoleum, took their places and waited for President Chun. Major Zin Bo, the leader of the group, was waiting at Wizaya Cinema (now CB Bank). He listened to the voices from the recorders which had been set up together with the bombs, thought that President Chun was already there and pressed the button.

At that moment, I was at a friend's house in Myinmo Street. Hearing the bomb blast, I was shocked. In all, a total of 16 people died, including

Daw Aung San Suu Kyi with flowers basket before sending to Martyr's Mausoleum on July 18, 1998 evening.

the South Korean foreign minister, other ministers, deputy ministers and security personnel. From the Myanmar side, some people from the news and information department, a cameraman from a documentary film and some security men died. (The cameraman was photographer U Tin Kyaing from *Kye-Mon* Daily, the father of my friend.)

Their mission accomplished, the North Korean spies left for Thakutwa village near the sea. A submarine was waiting, but if they could not get there in time, they planned to commit suicide. Major Zin Bo was arrested at Thida Jetty while he was trying to go along Pazundaung creek to the sea. He tried to kill himself by exploding a hand grenade, but it only damaged his eyes and cut one of his hands. Near Thakutwa village, Capt. Kim Min-Chul was arrested. Sin Ki Chu committed suicide.

The court sentenced Major Zin Bo and Capt. Kim Min-Chul to death, but they were never executed. Whistle-blower Kim Min-Chul was freed and handed over to the government of South Korea. Zin Bo was kept in a separate house in Insein Prison until 2000. I saw him there from 1989 to 1990. I was disgusted to see the man who destroyed Martyr's Mausoleum and degraded our country in the international arena. Even though I hate him, though, there are still people who worship Zin Bo and his masters.

(They hanged Ohn Kyaw Myint and Salaing Tin Maung Oo, but spared the life of Zin Bo. We shall never forgive and forget until the end of the world!)

The roof of the building was blown out by the bomb-blast and some of the tombs were damaged, but it could have been repaired and restored to its original plan. I don't know why it was demolished and re-constructed in a new design. (I've known of their belief that nothing that reminds people of the past should be restored to its original state ever since the house of U Phar and Daw Suu, Bogyoke's parents, was destroyed by fire.)

Now, the public are not allowed to go in and observe closely, and from a distance you cannot distinguish which tomb is whose because it is built with an open-air design. I hadn't been there since 1983, so my first visit to the mausoleum in its new design was in 2011. I was anxious to pay homage to Bogyoke Aung San's tomb, but I was only allowed to do it from 20 feet away, and the tombs themselves are no longer the way they used to be. Now they are placed in a line. You can see a big star on one which is supposed to be Bogyoke Aung San's. This is the story of how the old Martyrs' Mausoleum came to be destroyed and a new one appeared in its place.

Recently, when South Korean President Lee Myung-bak was on an official visit to Yangon, he went to Arzani Hill and saluted the South Korean citizens who were killed there in 1983. He was believed to bow to our martyrs also. I am not sure if North Korean criminal Zin Bo is still in Insein prison or not, but our historic Martyrs' Mausoleum was lost because of him.

The other day I found a cartoon in a journal very amusing. In this cartoon, two men were talking.

One man said, "Those are not included, I hope."

The other one asked, "Which ones?"

The first one replied, "Of course, Shwedagon Pagoda and Martyrs' Mausoleum."

I like this cartoon very much. It's worth worrying about, the way all the state-owned buildings and land-plots have fallen into the hands of cronies. The cartoonist seems to be concerned about it too. Everybody feels the same way. In the city of Yangon, the only public properties left are Resistance Park, Arzarni Hill, the *wuttaka-myay* (religious land) of Shwedagon Pagoda and the Yangon University campus. Even the area around the bronze statue of Bogyoke at Kandawgyi is shrinking. Bogyoke Aung San's statue complains that the noise from the Ferris wheel and the merry-go-round is disturbing. The markets all around the city of Yangon that have existed for generations are now feeling embarrassed because the cronies are eyeing them, and the cronies know nothing about national and cultural heritage. They only know how much profit they can get out of something and are trying to get hold of our national heritage sites for their own benefit, in collaboration with corrupt officials who misuse their authority. In this way, hundreds of national heritages have been lost.

The charity of the cronies is nothing considering the state-owned property they have got. They have wiped out government-owned

Daw Aung San Suu Kyi paying obeisance to her father Bogyoke Aung San's tomb at the Martyrs' Mausoleum on the Martyr's Day in 2012.

buildings, residential plots of land, land grabbed from the tillers and farmers and forests. In comparison with what they took, the donations they made amounted to nothing. So the cartoonist's worry is reasonable.

Arzarni Hill is owned by the Ministry of Culture. On west Shwegondine Road, from the start of Arzani Street (in front of the M3 Food Centre) to Yedashe Lanthit, the land has been like a forest lane for many years. It was quite appropriate that the Ministry of Culture built apartments for the families of their staff there, but under the pretext of religious causes they also built shops to rent. The shops go for K300,000 a month or K3.6 million a year. It is not nice to see bars and beer pubs with satellite dishes installed on the fence-poles of the compound of Martyr's Mausoleum. Heaps of garbage and black-market fuel sellers along the road leading to the pagoda disgrace the holy place.

Arzarni Hill is the northern continuation of Theinguttra Hill. It has been here since the time of Lord Buddha, more than 2600 years ago. It is our cultural heritage, complete with natural beauty that we must value and preserve.

Dear Thamee Shwewar, I don't know if Martyrs' Day this year will be different from previous years. I saw a new concrete platform with kha-ye (star-flower) trees all along the fence of the Arzarni Hill compound. It would be good if the public were allowed to pay tribute to the *Arzarnis* freely. All schools, including private schools, should go to Martyrs' Mausoleum to pay respect to the *Arzarnis* on Martyrs' Day.

When you study the modern history of Myanmar, you will learn about Bogyoke Aung San, founder of the Tatmadaw, Chief of Staff of the Armed Forces and our national leader. His birthday is February 13, 1915, and he died on July 19, 1947, which is now Arzarni Day. All the students of your school should go on an excursion tour to Bogyoke Museum on Tower Lane Street and to the Bogyoke statue in Kandawgyi Park so as not to forget Bogyoke Aung San.

A friend of mine was born on February 13, the same as Bogyoke. He used to do meritorious deeds on his birthday and used to say how he wished to be a politician like Thakhin Aung San.

Thamee Shwewar, will you go to Martyr's Mausoleum and salute the *Arzarnis* on Arzarni Day?

(To Shwewaryaung, daughter of Jimmy and Nilar Thein)

– *Open News (Vol. 4, No. 38, July 2012)*

The two grandsons of the national hero

Ama has two sons. The elder son is Maung Myint San Aung, aka Alexander, and the younger one is Maung Htein Lin, aka Kim. Maung Myint San Aung was born on Thursday, April 12, 1973. Maung Htein Lin was born on Saturday, September 24, 1977. Up until 1996 the sons were under their mother's close motherly supervision. Now they are living far apart from their loving mother, though sometimes they come back to her again. The motherly spirit she bears toward her sons will never recede. When the right time arrived, each son was noviciated into the Buddhist order. Although her sons now live in a foreign land, meritorious deeds in Buddhist fashion are still performed on their birthdays.

Whatever *Ama* does for her sons, strict equality is always been on her mind. She always treats her two sons equally and she never tolerates anyone putting one before the other. I have often been blamed for doing so myself. It was my fault, because I cannot keep from being swayed by the personalities of the people who come to be in touch with me. I used to say, "This person is the only one who will do for me."

Allow me to relate something. One of *Ama*'s friends paid her a visit once. You have probably heard of his ancestor, who used to sign his name with "(Burma)" attached to it. The visitor was one of the twin grandsons of the great Lord Mountbatten (Burma). It was nearly 15 years ago and I myself fail to remember it well, but I remember that he wanted to give me two T-shirts as presents.

Ama called me and said, "KMS, he is one of the twin grandsons of Lord Mountbatten of Burma and his name is Tim. He was nearby when Lord Mountbatten was assassinated by a bomb attack. One of his eyes went blind in the attack. He's my friend. He told me that he saw you always wearing the T-shirt with my portrait on it during his visits here. So he wanted to give T-shirts to you. His T-shirts do not bear my portraits. They are only ordinary T-shirts. He asked me to enquire whether you are willing to accept them, so I am asking you about it."

"I don't want to accept if there is no portrait of you on them," I told her.

She said, "You don't have to be that way. Accept them, please."

So I accepted them and told him I was thankful for the presents. Then as soon as *Ama*'s friend went back I told her, "*Ama*, please give these two T-shirts to Kim." With a solemn look she told me, "KMS, you're awfully partial. I gave birth to two sons and you should give one to each of them. If they are to be given to Kim only you are not being just." So I had to make amends for my words.

Now I hope you understand that *Ama* prefers things to be fair and square. I love Maung Htein Lin a bit too much. You might have heard that he was referred to as "Htein Lin!" in the song. Beside the fact that he is the youngest, his facial contours and character traits, which are so similar to *Ama*'s, plus his frequent visits endeared him to all of us. We love both of them equally but Maung Myint San Aung's aloofness made us sometimes feel somewhat strange with him.

Oh! I've committed another fresh impartial act unwittingly. I am certain *Ama* would blame me with a solemn face.

Recently I placed a birthday wish for Maung Htein Lin in the ad column of The Myanmar Times. Please don't let *Ama* learn of the ad! If ever she learned of the ad she would surely say, "KMS, you are very partial. Why didn't you send an ad to the journals on Maung Myint San Aung's birthday earlier?" I am quite sure that nobody but I am to be blamed.

I always tried to be fair. The instant *Ama* told me, "KMS, tomorrow is Myint San Aung's birthday," I replied, "Don't worry, *Ama*. On his birthday I will offer the number of yellow roses exactly equivalent in number to his age plus one, and the same number of cups of water to the Buddha at the Thursday corner (the western corner) of Shwedagon Pagoda. Gold leaf donations will be offered to the pagoda trustees' office."

Then, when *Ama* said, "KMS, tomorrow is Htein Lin's birthday," I told her not to worry. On the day I offered to the Buddha the number of red roses (plus one) and the number of cups of water (plus one) that were exactly equivalent in number to his age at the Saturday corner (the southwestern corner) of the Shwedagon Pagoda. Also, I offered donations for gold leaf through the pagoda trustees' office. I tried to be fair and square, *Ama*.

Ama has the kind of love that every mother has for her children, but her determination that, for the sake of the country and of the people, one should be ready to give up one's family belongs to her alone. She is proud of her sons, who, though their mother failed in her motherly duty, still understand her difficulty and poignant plight completely.

The family, during their occasional reunions, always tried to recapture their relationship with amazing wholeheartedness, despite the duration of their absences. The mother and her younger son went on a pilgrimage tour to Bagan together with a little bodyguard, a dog named Taichido. While in Bagan I'm sure she would have told the story of King Kyansittha. She would surely have told her son about the king's promise to his son and also the son Raja Kumar's reciprocating *metta* for his father. Historical evidence of their relationship still abounds and is there for everyone to see. Good evidence is always intact.

Unlike in the past, the mother and son, now together again, leave a beautiful image for the people here. Talk of the son's facial curves being the exact likeness of his mother's kept ringing in our ears. So I composed a little poem:

This son's face is contoured

In the likeness of his loving mother's,

She's the daughter created in the image of her father.

Dr. Michael Aris and Daw Aung San Suu Kyi

request the pleasure of the company of

- -

at the

Shinbyu Ceremony of their Sons

Maung Myint San Aung

(Alexander)

and

Maung Htein Lin

(Kim)

at 54-56 University Avenue, Rangoon
on Saturday, the 11th Day of the Waxing
Moon of Pyatho 1348 B.E. (10.1.87)
From 9:00 am to 1:00 pm
(Devotions: 11:30 am)

ရှင်ပြုအလှူတော်မင်္ဂလာ စိတ်ကြားလွှာ

• • • •

ကျေးဇူးရှင် မိဘ များဖြစ်ကြသော
ဗိုလ်ချုပ်အောင်ဆန်း - ဒေါ်ခင်ကြည် တို့အား အမွှန်းပြုလျက်
ရန်ကုန်မြို့၊ အမှတ် ၅၄-၅၆ တက္ကသိုလ်ရိပ်သာလမ်း နေ
Dr. Michael Aris - ဒေါ်အောင်ဆန်းစုကြည်
တို့က သံသရာဝဋ် ဆင်းရဲမှ ကင်းငြိမ်းရာ နိဗ္ဗာန်ကိုရည်သန်လျက်
ရင်နှစ်သည်းချာ သားလှရတနာ များဖြစ်ကြသော

မောင်မြင့်ဆန်း၊ အောင် (Alexander)

နှင့်

မောင်ထိန်လင်း (Kim)

တို့အား ရှင်သာမကော အဖြစ်သွတ်သွင်းချီးမြင့်
အလှူဒါန ပြုလုပ်မည် ဖြစ်ပါ၍
၁၃၄၈ ခု၊ ပြာသိုလဆန်း ၁၁ ရက် (၁၀-၁-၁၉၈၇) စနေနေ့
နံနက်(၉း၀၀) နာရီ မှ မွန်းလွဲ (၁း၀၀) နာရီ ထိ
အထက်ပါ နေအိမ်သို့ ပရိတ်တရားတော်နာဘို့၊
ကုသိုလ်အမျှယူရန် ကြ ရောက်ပါ မည့်အ ကြောင်း၊
ခင်မင်လေးစားစွာ ဖိတ်ကြားအပ်ပါသည်။

The invitation card for the *Shinbyu* (Noviciation) ceremony of two grandsons of Bogyoke Aung San

And she has given birth to the son who is the image of her own self.

The son left for his mother a little bodyguard dog named Taichido.

What a son! Oh! Mummy's son, the unsurpassed son.

Since *Ama* has already noviciated her two sons into the Buddhist order, all that is left for them to do is to be ordained into Buddhist monkhood. I am looking forward to the time when both of them happen to be here again and can be ordained as Buddhist monks by their loving mother, so that she can be worthy of being addressed as a *rahan amah* (mother of a monk).

Then we will really miss our brother Michael, who left us forever.

– The Myanmar Times (Vol. 28, No. 542)

Daughter of the father of the Tatmadaw

Just after midnight on May 3, 2008, Cyclone Nargis struck Yangon. Although the Weather Bureau had given prior warnings, people failed to take them seriously enough because of a lack of experience. Only after 11pm on May 2 did they start to feel the extent of the storm.

After 1am the roof of my home started peeling off because of the upthrust of the strong winds. By 3am the tin roofing of the house was totally gone. I've never experienced such catastrophic winds in all my life. We could do nothing but sit helplessly and look on with great worry and with tears streaming down our faces. We also had to be mindful of the danger of the beams crashing down onto our heads.

Soon my home looked like an open-air building. Living under it became impossibility, but leaving would also be difficult due to the power failure and the darkness outside. The rain became heavier and the wind very forceful. We decided to leave our house in the morning as soon as it became light. At 6am we left the house. We found the floodwaters on the road reached our lower thighs. It couldn't be helped, so we forced ourselves onward through the water with the aim of finding a house that could offer us temporary shelter.

Ama was under house arrest at the time. My catering duty could not be interrupted under any circumstances; I needed to arrive at the exact time every morning and every evening without fail. Ama is a woman of great exactitude. I wondered what had become of her home!

When I came to the end of the road, a friend at *Shwe-U-Daung* (peacock) haircutters shouted, "Hi! Are you on your way there? The trees have been uprooted and overhead power lines have been cut, and there are loose ends lying all over the rain-soaked ground. There is no way of passing through the storm-devastated debris. Stay here a while and continue after the rain has stopped." So I took shelter in his home for a short while.

At about 11am, the rain lessened somewhat and I left again. As I walked on I saw uprooted trees in every direction. There were no sign of buses moving about. Thiri Mingalar Market is an important wholesale market so I thought cars were bound to be there. I headed for the market. Because of the uprooted trees and loose ends of power lines lying about on the ground, I got to the market only after nearly half an hour's walk. No line buses or rental cars were to be found. I saw only one diplomatic limousine and three or four private cars. Many people were taking shelter there.

After midday the rain totally stopped and you could see a little bit of sunlight. I could think of no way to continue my journey ahead. I walked up the road determined to face whatever came my way. Passing low-lying tree trunks and naked copper wires lying loose all about the ground, I walked across the bridge in front of the Hwa Kyone High School in Kyimyindine, crossed Shan Road, Baho Road, Shinsawpu Road, Dhamma Zedi Road and Link Road, and walked along west Shwe Gondaing until finally I reached the front of NLD headquarters. The landlord there and his family entreated me, saying they had already tried to reach Ama's house but found the road impassable, with uprooted trees lying low above the ground in every direction. They advised me to accept the blame for staying here today and only go tomorrow. So I slept there for the night. I hate Nargis! I will never forget Cyclone Nargis that came in May 2008.

The next morning at 8 o'clock I walked along Kaba Aye Pagoda Road. When I reached the Kokkine Road intersection and tried to walk along Kokkine Road I felt as if I was passing through a deep forest. When I got near the front gate of Ama's house, the great *kokko* tree

Daw Aung San Suu Kyi (middle), elder son Maung Myint San Aung (left) and younger son Maung Htein Lin Aung (right)

that stood on one side of the gate was uprooted and lying along the front fence of her house, thus making the entrance into her compound difficult. The huge *kokko* tree in the middle of her compound was also uprooted. The meshed bamboo walls that served as fences around her compound were also lying flat on the ground.

I entered the compound and called to Aunty Win. When she came she asked me why I hadn't come yesterday, and said that Ama had enquired about the condition of my house.

I told Aunty Win about all the things that had happened to me.

She told me, "KMS, your sister (Ama) said that her compound is in very bad shape. Most of the slates have fallen from the roof and the house is wet through with rainwater. She wanted help from Dr Tin Myo Win's brother who is a building contractor. I had to contact Doctor Tin Myo Win immediately and made all the necessary arrangements for repairs. Because water has become the number one priority, we rushed about and bought purified water bottles first. In the meantime, Dr Tin Myo Win arrived and made necessary arrangements for repair work."

"All the trees along the lakefront have fallen. All the white mango trees that Ama's mother planted have fallen. Ama will surely feel sad. What makes her sadder still is the unfortunate plights of Nargis victims from Ayeyarwady Division and Yangon Division."

Although Ama could not go there herself and make donations, she gave me some bales of clothing for the victims, saying, "KMS, donate them to anyone you want." If somebody were to ask me about the things I did and the things I learned about Nargis victims, I would have answers ready for them. I donated the clothing that had been handed to me to a poet and an editor with my own hands.

On May 6, 2008, the home repairmen entered the compound and started their repair work. Although the debris-clearing volunteers performed their work meticulously, because of the size of the workload they were unable to cope. So the authorities lent their helping hands. On the morning of May 20, 2008, at 10am, seven officers and 63 servicemen, plus two chainsaws, came along and did the clearing job.

Ama took full responsibility for catering. She prepared 100 bottles of soft drinks and 100 boxes of biryani, plus 60 more boxes which were left as a reserve.

Ama said, "KMS, young *yebaws* (soldiers) eat their breakfast at 10am. Bring the biryani here by 9am sharp." She had watched them every day and remembered their routines. By 10:30am Ama could be seen distributing the biryani boxes among the *yebaws* herself. Aunty Win brought boxes for the officers who were standing near me. She told me, "KMS, three of us plus you will have our breakfasts together later. She says she had set aside four boxes for us."

At 1pm when it was Ama's mealtime, Aunty Win brought a biryani box for me. She said, "KMS, our sister says that the four biryani boxes she kept for us turned out to be reserve boxes with no chicken inside. We're going to eat plain biryani with fried prawn *balachaungs*. She asked whether it will be alright for you."

I replied, "Yes, it's quite OK."

When I tried to eat the plain biryani with fried prawn *balachaungs*, I found it unappetising. Biryani being not in the list of foods I like best, I left it mostly untouched. After Aunty Win came back and saw the opened uneaten box, she seemed to enjoy reporting the matter to Ama.

The next time she entered she told me, "KMS, our sister made the bread she kept ready into sandwiches. She asked me to tell you to eat them if you don't like the biryani."

"Oh, Aunty Win, I can eat outside at the restaurants. Why bother about me? Why do you report everything to Ama?"

She replied, "Our sister asked you to eat them. Finish it up, will you?"

Ama always looks kindly on her inferiors. We saw she didn't at all mind eating the plain biryani that had been put aside accidentally.

That afternoon she wanted to treat the young *yebaws* with tea-mix and biscuits. She told me, "KMS, buy me some tea-mix and a tin of biscuits," and handed me some old mildewed K500 notes. When I replied that she should keep her old notes and that I would go back home and fetch some new notes for the purpose, she told me not to go back because there was no time. She insisted on me going straight away with the notes she had handed me. So I bought the things she asked me to buy. She treated the young *yebaws* with tea-mix and biscuits at 3pm. She had talked warmly to the Tatmadaw men that morning while welcoming them under her portico, and she also said farewell warmly when they left.

The scene of the loving daughter of the father of Myanmar's armed forces warmly welcoming the Tatmadaw men on their arrival and saying goodbye to them on their departure filled my heart with ecstatic happiness.

– The Myanmar Times (Vol. 27, No. 540-541)

Aung San Suu Kyi, who inherited the nursing spirit from her mother

Ama's mother was a nurse. During the Japanese occupation, her father was sick and had to be admitted to what was then known as Rangoon General Hospital. Dr Ba Than was head of the hospital at that time. His daughter Kitty, aka Daw Khin May Than, worked at her father's hospital as a nurse. Among the nurses in the hospital were Daw Khin Gyee (elder sister of Ama's mother and Thakhin Than Tun's wife), Daw Khin Kyi (Bogyoke Aung San's wife) and Kitty Ba Than (Bogyoke Ne Win's wife). Incidentally, it is a wonder that these three nurses all became well-known figures in Myanmar politics later on.

Ama's father fell in love with her mother while he was in the hospital and eventually they got married. Karen nationalist leader Saw San Po Thin and his comrades composed the following song dedicated to their marriage:

Let me swear by the silvery light of the moon that shines above that

I've never been in love with any woman but you, oh, Sayama

The song will never grow stale in Myanmar people's hearts. It will remain forever fresh as the first flakes of snow.

After Myanmar's independence, Ama's mother was appointed departmental head of the Maternity and Welfare Department as well as leader of the Myanmar Nurses' Association and the Myanmar Women's Association. She was also eventually honoured with an appointment as the first woman ambassador, to India and Ceylon (now Sri Lanka). After 1962 she led a relatively quiet life and in 1967 she retired from her ambassadorial post. She was given a remuneration of K1000 per month for being the wife of an *arzarni*.

56 University Avenue
Rangoon
Dated: 3-1-78

To

U Than Htut
General Manager
Five Star Line Corporation
Rangoon

At Rajgiri in India a Bogyoke Aung San *Tipitaka* Library has been established in a Myanmar monastery. For the library we are sending four boxes of books (4 boxes) comprising 169 books. The cost of the books is K1,127.

The books have been approved by the Ministry of Trade to be sent abroad. I would like to request your kind approval to send four boxes of books by steamship to Calcutta per the kind request of Rajgiri Sayadaw.

Signed,

(Daw Khin Kyi, wife of Bogyoke Aung San)

(English translation of Daw Khin Kyi's request to the Five Star Shipping Line)

၅၆ တက္ကသိုလ် ရိပ်သာ
ရန်ကုန်မြို့။
နေ့စွဲ၊ ၃ - ၁ - ၇၀။

သို့
ဦး သန်း ထွတ်
အရှေ့ ဆွေမှန် နေရာ၁။
ကြယ်ပြဲ ပွင့်သ ဘော၁ ကော၁ ပို့ ရေး ၂င်း ။
ရန်ကုန်မြို့။

အိန္ဒိယပြည် ၇၁ဇ ကြိုက်မြို့၊ မြန်မာ၁ ပိုင် ကျောင်း ၌ နိုင်ချပ် အောင်ဆန်း ပိဋကတ်တိုက် ဖွင့်ထား ပါသည်။ ၄င်း အဖွက်စ၁အုပ် သေတ္တ၁၊ လေး သေတ္တ၁ (၄/ သေတ္တ၁) စ၁အုပ် ၄၇ (၁၆၉) အုပ်၊ တန်ဘိုး ၄၄မ၁ ၁၁၂ ၇ိ/ - ဖြစ် ပါသည်။

၄င်း စ၁အုပ်များ ကို ကုန်သွယ် ရေး ဝန်ကြီး ၄၁န မှ ခွင့်ပြုသ၁း ပြီး ဖြစ် ပါသည်။ ၄င်း စ၁အုပ် သေတ္တ၁ လေး သေတ္တ၁ ကို အိန္ဒိယ (ကလကတ္တ၁ မြို့သို့) သ ဘော၁ တင်ပို့ ခွင့်ပြုပါ ပါ ရန်/ ၇၁ဇ ကြိုက်ဆ ရ၁ တော်၏ မေတ္တ၁ ရပ်ခံ ချက်အ ရ၊ မေတ္တ၁ ရပ်ခံ အပ် ပါသည်။

(နိုင်ချပ်က ဒေါ် ၆ေၐ T ခ င်ကြည်)

(Myanmar version of Daw Khin Kyi's request to the Five Star Shipping Line)

Ama's mother was the president of the Myanmar Nurses' Association. When we grew up, Kitty Ba Than was the president. Another colleague of Ama's mother was Ms Eileen Barbro. She was a matron when the famous heart-to-heart conjoined twins Ma Nan Soe and Ma Nan San were successfully operated on by a team of Myanmar surgeons. During the SLORC regime, I remember Ms Barbro being appointed president of the Myanmar Nurses' Association with great pomp and ceremony.

While I have never seen first-hand how Ama's mother led her life with strict discipline, I learned about it from reading the notes and memos she jotted down.

In 1995 when Ama was set free from internment I returned to her service along with with Ko Htein, Ko Aung and Ko Aung Kyaw Oo and did my allotted duty together with her cousins. I had to take care of her day-to-day meals. I worked together with her relatives such as Ko Ko Nyi (U Aye Win), Ko Htwe (Ko Htwe Win), Ma Ma Lay (Ko Htwe Win's wife), Cho Cho (Ko Cho Aung Than), Ko Aung Kyaw Oo (a maternal relative) and Ko Aung (son of Bo Min Lwin, one of Bogyoke Aung San's bodyguards).

I used to get up very early and go to the Hledan market to buy vegetables, meat, fish and eggs to prepare the daily meals for Ama and the rest of us. One day when I arrived back at about 8am I saw the others burning a large heap of assorted documents, notebooks and posters in front of the small kitchen beside the water stand. After hastily dropping the things I had brought back from the market, I turned to look at the blaze and saw Ama's old snapshots, large and small posters bearing her picture, her documents and some books with untidy notes and memos inside.

Ama had asked them to be reduced to flames because of their growing volume. As I had just come back from my daily trip to the Hledan market, however, I did not know they were doing this with Ama's consent. So I told them angrily, "You're obliterating history. These are documents we have to preserve for future use. They're priceless documents!" and so on and so forth. So Ko Htwe, Ko Aung Kyaw Oo, Cho Cho and Ko Bo Soe Tint (ex-*Voice of Myanmar employee*) replied, "Will you please stop yelling at us? You take whatever you would like to take and save them if you like. We're not doing this of our own free will. We burnt them because Ama told us to do so. If you don't believe us you can go and ask Ama yourself." So I tried to contain my anger and take whatever I thought was worth saving. I fished out from the blazing fire some posters containing Ama's portrait and some documents and notebooks that had not yet been burnt.

Later, when I scrutinised what I had saved from the flames, I saw among them a notebook that contained Ama's mother's daily shopping notes, with special accounts for days such as Martyrs' Day, and another book in which each day she had listed the guests that paid a visit to her house. I also found a notebook into which she had copied some religious literature and sermons, and also Queen Elizabeth's family album from 1954-1955. At the time I only valued the painted posters with Ama's portrait on them and the rest were of little interest to me. Later, when I read the notebooks written in Ama's mother's own handwriting, I came to realise that she had followed a disciplined way of life and that these were really important notes. I kept them very carefully, but when Cyclone Nargis came, most of them went along with it. The discipline Ama has now is as great as her mother's was. She is heir to her father's political prowess and to her mother's disciplined way of life and motherly love.

When she started organising the NLD in 1988, I joined as a member and was given membership recruiting duty with recruiting order No. Hta/147/Cee/88. The twin daughters of ex-Minister Saw San Po Thin, Aunty Ruth and Aunty Rose, were the first members from Kyimyindine Township whom I had the honour of recruiting into the NLD. Daw Hlawaddy was also recruited. Their membership cards were processed and handed over to the Kyimyindine NLD. Because I was a roving organiser, I was recruiting members from various townships. I also recruited Ma San San Win who lived next door to my house. Our township had 11 wards, so the other 10 people who received recruiting orders said that they were forming a township organising committee with 11 recruiting order holders including me. I would be the only one out of the 11 organisers who belonged to the NLD. The other 10 were from U Aung Gyi's party. Among the other 10, one believed in Ama. During the 1988 demonstrations he had helped Ama's cause, along with the Nay Oak (St. Paul) group. He cooperated with me and his name is Ko Tin Oo.

He allowed our party to open its office in his apartment. When the NLD split with U Aung Gyi's party he decided to remain with us. We reorganised the NLD with those who remained. Ko Tin Oo was elected president and was a recruiting organiser. I also had to take care of the youth. Maung Myo Nyunt, who is a youth organiser now, has been with us since he was a young man. When it was decided that youth affairs works were to be started from Yangon, Win Hlaing (1990 hluttaw representative, now in the USA), Johnny aka Myint Soe (now in the USA), Nay Win (hluttaw representative), Mg Mg Oo (now part of Ama's security detail), Thet Khine, Aung Myint (Auzar), Yan Aung (Mg Karlu) and I started our work together. We continued our organising work in the states and divisions. Some of the people listed above have since left their work but Maung Myo Nyunt, Ko Nay Win and Maung Maung Oo are still in place.

Lawyer Daw San San Win was the pupil of Yangon Division organiser U Tun Tint (Han Thar Tun, the father of Han Min Set). U Tun Tin asked me not to leave her out, so I arranged for her to become a member also.

On June 22, 1989, Ama planned to come to our office to talk to the public. The day before there had been a shooting incident that killed one person at Myaynigone when Ama was attending the anniversary of Myaynigone Day, and she had been taken from there in a TE-11 truck by Col Tha Htay, No. 3 Area Commander of Yangon, and brought to the SLORC office in Sangyaung township, from whence they let her go back home. Because of that incident we were worried about her planned visit. In our township there had been security movements and curtailments since the previous evening.

It was my job to make Ama's visit here possible. I had to consult with president Ko Tin Oo and Ko Myo Nyunt. The portable barricades were being kept ready at strategic points of the roads so that they could be used to control public traffic. In case the approach roads to the Yedwin Road NLD office were closed by barricades, we planned to let the public pass through the picket fences of the neighbouring houses that led to the office. I took on the responsibility of bringing Ama to the office myself. She had to be at the Yedwin Road office at

1pm on June 22. Her planned route would start at noon in Dr Myint Oo's Publica pickup along lower Kyimyintdine Road, then continue to Bagaya Road, to Myaynigone and Pyay roads, and then to University Avenue. Lower Kyimindine Road was closed at the traffic lights at the Bagaya intersection. Bagaya Road was closed at the Myaynigon traffic lights. I told Ama about our situation. She decided to carry on as planned.

We drove along lower Kyimindine Road heading south. When we came to the traffic lights at the bottom of the Bagaya banks the road was blocked and our motorcade was stopped. They asked to see the person responsible and so I went to see the officer. There I insisted that Daw Aung San Suu Kyi was in the motorcade heading for the Ahlone township NLD office and that I took responsibility for the trip. They finally allowed us to go on but I was asked to give them a list of people riding in the motorcade. The roads were deserted, but there were signs of people peeping out to watch us pass. We saw two military trucks driving along. When we arrived in front of the Ahlone post office, the traffic policeman directed us toward upper Forest Road. When I told him that the Yaydwin Road NLD office was in front of us and we were heading there, and also that Daw Suu was with us, he contacted the higher authorities for orders. We were kept waiting there for some time. He asked for the name of the person who was responsible and I gave my name to him.

On our arrival the length and breadth of Yaydwin Road was teeming with crowds. They moved the barricades to let in Ama's vehicle. The other vehicles were left wherever they happened to be. Ama gave her speech. The speech was an attack against those in power. Then the township SLORC came and summoned me by name for the first time. I went up the road and told them that while Ama was still here I was not ready to come. I promised them I would go to the office after Ama left for home. Again I was summoned to appear at No. 3 Area Commander's office in Yangon. I told them that I could only go there after Ama had left for home.

We consulted among ourselves. I was to be arrested. What were we going to do? When they let a crowd of people board Dr Myint Oo's van I crouched in the middle so that I could not be seen from outside. I gave them the slip by staying in the middle of the crowded car until we arrived back into Ama's compound. When I told Ama about the summons she asked me to go see them. I could not let them arrest me and so I went into hiding. When they could not arrest me, however, they took Ko Tin Oo. I let Ma San San Win take over my role and arranged everything so that her job would be smooth and easy. I was arrested in Ama's compound on July 20 and brought to the Interrogation Department on July 22 and 23. They set president Ko Tin Oo free and I was interrogated in connection with the June 21 public speech Ama had made.

On May 27, 1990, Ma San San Win was elected as a hluttaw representative. I was also freed from detention. Because the representatives were attending a conference in Mandalay I accompanied Ma San San Win there and came back to Yangon afterward. Ma San San Win was then accused of conducting a meeting with the purpose of forming a shadow government at U Ba Bwa's house in Amarapura. She was imprisoned for crimes against the state. I had to help her family see her in prison. She was set free in 1994.

When Ama gained her freedom in 1995, we made celebration in her compound. The celebrations were mostly arranged by a group of women which included Ma San San Win. I introduced them to Ama and she greatly appreciated their dedication to party works. The full names of the ladies in the group all end with Win. The group includes Khin Khin Win, Tin Tin Win, San San Win, Kyin Kyin Win and Tin Tin Win Maung.

Ma San San Win was suspected of having cervix cancer but she treated the affliction with her typical nonchalance. Only in 1999, when Ama insisted she should have a consultation with Dr Tin Myo Win, was she officially diagnosed with cervix cancer. Dr Tin Myo Win told Ama about his findings although he kept them a secret from Ma San San Win.

From the first day Ma San San Win was hospitalised, Ama went to the Bar Street hospital each day at 4pm, after her office hours. She went there not just to see the patient but also to nurse her and comfort her, as if she were a kindly nurse, and she used to return home only after 6pm. She kept going there, always on time and without fail, up until Ma San San Win's last breath. Ama showed devotion until the final hours of Ma San San Win's life and displayed the camaraderie and nursing spirit she inherited from her mother. She attended Ma San San Win's funeral procession and also visited her home and comforted her family members.

(Dedicated to our colleague Ma San San Win)

Ama's bodyguard, the little Taichido

I first wrote this story haphazardly a long time ago, thinking I would make it into a fair copy when the time was ripe. I think it was during December 2011. Dr Tin Myo Win made a vinyl picture of himself together with a little dog with the caption "Beware of dog". On close scrutiny it turned out that the little dog was Taichido. I smiled to myself. It must have been Ama's idea.

This story was first written after that moment. Later I added a little bit here and there and the story came into being. Quite recently Ama wrote something herself about little Taichido and, being somewhat knowledgeable about the subject myself, it gave me an itch to say something too.

When Ama was a child, the little animal with which she was most familiar was a cat raised by her grandfather which he called "pussy-cat". The grandchildren venerated it and called it "grandpa-cat".

When Ama came of age, the family moved to New Delhi, India, where her mother was working. Because of the high society they moved about in there, she had to learn horseback riding. After her grandfather's cat, her second pets were therefore colts and fillies.

She started learning to ride with a little horse named "Black Prince".

Later horses were "Privy Raja" and "Shivaji". During that part of her life she befriended many young animals, but that wasn't the end of her friendship with them.

During 1969-1970, when she worked for the United Nations, she grew attached to a little dog named "NP" which Dora Than Aye raised in her home. For Ama and Aunty, NP was all they cared about. NP used to make the guests who sat on the sofas at their home miserable. It was NP's indelible trait.

After Ama got married to our brother Michael they lived in Bhutan. There they reared a brown-and-white-haired little dog which they called "Puppy". It used to go to bed with its front paws hugging Ama's neck. It also used to wrestle with the shoes and woolen socks our brother left around. Along with the rest of Ama's family, Puppy traveled around the world quite often. It went to places like Bhutan, Nepal, Yangon and England. It looked after the family's children up until the time when they had grown big and tall. Everyone in the family loved it. It grew to be the family's mascot. When Ama came back to Myanmar in 1988 she was separated from Puppy as well as from her loving family. Puppy undoubtedly missed Ama and Ama would have also felt the same about it. In 1991, when Ama's freedom was not yet in sight, Puppy died at the age of 19, which is quite old for a dog. Ama's attachment to the family dog probably made her rather sad. That is the way of every living being.

You have probably seen Puppy's picture. In journals published after August 2011 you sometimes saw a picture of an elderly lady with a scarf tied around her neck hugging a huge dog. That huge dog was Puppy. In the journals then they wrote that Ama lived together with two women and a dog, which was incorrect. She lived with two women, all right, but not with a dog.

On August 11, 2009, Ama was sentenced to one-and-a-half years of house confinement. They had arrested her on May 13, 2009, and therefore the one-and-a-half years would be up in November 2010. We welcomed her back on November 13, 2010.

Maung Htein Lin, Ama's younger son, had been in Bangkok since the first week of November in expectation of her release. He had been separated from his mother for nearly ten years. He had last seen her in

2001. He was allowed to enter Myanmar on November 20, but Ama was so busy then that mother and son had no time to be alone together. So Dr Tin Myo Win had to show him around. On November 27 or 28, when the boy and Sayar (Dr. Tin Myo Win) went out together, Maung Htein Lin asked Sayar to take him to a young pups shop. He said he wanted to buy a young pup that would serve as a bodyguard for his mother.

On his return Ama saw him with a one-month-old pup.

Maung Htein Lin said, "This is your bodyguard, Mom," and extended the pup into his mother's hands. Because her son knew almost everything about the needs of his mother, she had to accept his offer affectionately.

The little pup was short-legged with an elongated body and reddish-

Maung Htein Lin bought little-Taichido; bodyguard for her mother in November 2010.

Daw Aung San Suu Kyi and her younger son Maung Htein Lin at the party hosted at the Labour Party Headquarters in London. (2012 Europe Trip)

brown hair. When Maung Htein Lin left for England in December the little pup bodyguard was left with her for consolation. After his farewell celebrations, snapshots of the little pup were often seen on the internet. His name was Taichido. Being a handpicked present of her son, and filling the vacuum left by the family's previous dog Puppy, Ama lavished it with affection. Being a young, lovely pup, naturally everybody else loved it too.

Ama set down a schedule for its daily feeding. In addition there were dos and don'ts as to the ingredients of the food it should be fed. For instance, it was never to be fed with raw bones. The ground meat had to be roasted for feeding. The roasted meat had to be mixed well with some thinly cut green lettuce leaves and boiled rice. Dogs love to keep gnawing at bones. Naturally Taichido, being a dog, used to come near the rubbish heap beside the sink and search for pieces of thrown-away bones and leftover food. It used to wander about often, out of one room and into another. It also used to watch with interest the cats eating their meals and sometimes it made small barks at them. It seemed to be asking why it had been left out while they were being fed, although it would never annoy them.

Ama reminded us the kitchen door was always to be kept closed to keep Taichido away. Taichido was always around her whenever she was having a meal. Because she was kind, we kept meatballs in a saucer for Taichido close at hand.

Although she was busy all the day, she spent her evenings with Taichido. She bought little balls for it and in her spare time let it play with them.

After its original owner, Maung Htein Lin, left, Taichido became much more attached to Ama and wouldn't let anybody else get near her. It growled at anybody who dared to approach Ama too closely. It grew into a lovely animal though.

Since it is almost always around her, it has become known to most people. It behaves in a style all its own. Sometimes Ama's car even has to be sent back home to fetch Taichido because visitors want to have a look at it. It loves riding in a car and is used to sitting up right in the front of the car. Every time Dr Tin Myo Win drives into Ama's compound, he has to drive Taichido once around without fail.

It's a popular and lucky little dog. When the US secretary of state came, she brought along presents for it. The owner of Air Force One also brought presents for it. Maybe that's the reason why it has become rather proud nowadays.

When Maung Htein Lin came back for a second visit, Ama took him to Bagan on a pilgrimage tour. Naturally Taichido went with them. It was rather happy to go along on the pilgrimage. Its photographs appeared on the front page of the journals.

Gradually it has grown into a large dog and has come of age. One day I was reading while lying on my back. Taichido was playfully walking past me time and again as usual, and suddenly it bit me lightly on my hand. It bit again many more times. So I thought, "Taichido is having teething trouble. Being of age, we'll have to do something for it."

Not long after, we found it had been biting one person after another. I became rather afraid myself, but I knew how Ama would react. She would say, "It's not the fault of the one that bites. It's the fault of the one who has been bitten. The one who annoys it will be bitten." It was left as a bodyguard for her and was acting quite dutifully, but it was also lonely and so naturally it was irritable. We should all understand the nature of a dog.

I wanted to put out an advertisement for Taichido: "Wanted: a mate for Taichido. Not an ordinary mate, but one with a good pedigree."

           – *The Myanmar Times (Vol. 30, No. 587, 2012)*

Tie a yellow ribbon round the *yuzana* tree

// "Transparency" and "transparent society" are very popular words today. In the same vein, transparent expressions of what one feels in one's heart of hearts can also be made today.

When reading the writings of Saya Ko Po Kyawt, Saya Htet Myet and Ko Thein Than Oo, who have written so transparently about their thoughts and feelings, I gained much knowledge and also much to remember.

Some years ago there was a song that said, "The past is not to be forgotten," but today we have almost forgotten it. No, we don't remember it anymore! We want to say what we still remember because it could also be forgotten that way.

It was on the night of May 13, 2009, and I remember it well. That morning I had transported some provisions and fresh rations to Ama's residence as usual. My diary for the day reads as follows:

May 13, 2009 (Wednesday)

Ama said that yesterday interrogations were made again. To gain our legal rights a lawyer must be consulted. She told us to arrange for contact with U Kyi Win immediately.

သက်ဆိုင်ရာသို့

၂၀၀၉-ခုနှစ်၊ ဇူလိုင်လ (၂၇) ရက်။

ကျွန်ုပ် ဒေါ်အောင်ဆန်းစုကြည် ၏ ရန်ကုန်မြို့၊ ဗဟန်းမြို့နယ်၊ တက္ကသိုလ်ရိပ်သာလမ်း အမှတ် (၅၄/၅၆)၊ နေအိမ် အိမ်ထောင်စုစာရင်းတွင် အောက်အမည်ပါသူအား ထည့်သွင်းပေးရန် သဘောတူညီကြောင်း ထောက်ခံပါသည်။

ဦးမြင့်စိုး (၁၂/လအန (နိုင်) ၀၄၈၀၁၀) (ဘ) ဦးအုန်းမောင်

၁၅၇၊ ၄၀ါလမ်း၊ ၄၃န္ဒရပ်ကွက်၊ အလုံမြို့နယ်။

(ဒေါ်အောင်ဆန်းစုကြည်)

A certificate written by Daw Aung San Suu Kyi from the Insein Prison that she agrees to the entry of my name in her family list card to enable me to gain legal access to her in prison.

At 10pm the area administrator from Special Branch sent for us. He took us to the home minister's office. We met U Ni there. Major Win Naing Tun and party told us that Ama had asked us to see her at 6am the next morning. Video camera shots were also taken.

U Kyi Win told us that he had got permission to come into the compound.

A list of daily provisions was sent.

Ama told us that a search of her house had been made for the second time.

That night I was taking a rest at my house when at about 10pm security officials suddenly appeared in a car and announced they had come to fetch me. They told me to follow them immediately because their superiors wanted to talk to me personally about an important matter. While I arranged my things to bring with me, I racked my brains to think what the important matter could be. They told me not to bring anything because they would be sending me back after I'd seen the officials. When I arrived, I found Ko Htay Aung there also, so I was confounded. Some time later the officials explained that we had been called there because Ama told them to tell us to see her the next morning at 6am.

They sent me back home. I kept thinking about the matter on my way back, but the answer failed to come my way. I continued thinking about it when I reached home but still found no answer. I could not sleep for the whole night. "Something must be happening," I thought, but whether good or bad, something to be happy about or something to be sorry about, I could not say.

I awoke after 5am. I hurried out and took a taxi, telling the driver to drive fast. I was already late. Ama has very punctual habits and if I was late she would surely be upset.

When there was no interrogation as usual on arrival, I felt joyful, thinking things would turn out well. When Aunty Win came out to open the doors she told me to go upstairs right away and see Ama. I ran all the way upstairs to her. When I arrived Ko Htay Aung was already there.

She said, "Listen, I will tell you both at the same time. I am entering a meditation centre called the Insein retreat." (She was referring to Insein Prison). "They will come here to fetch me at 7am. If my entry at the retreat happens to be a long-term one, KMS will have to supply me with provisions as usual. To make your trips to me lawful you must apply to have your name entered on my family list card. Both of you shall look after my house. Ma Ni and Ko Htin Kyaw will also visit from time to time.

(English translation of Daw Aung San Suu Kyi's letter)

To whom it many concern

24 July 2009

This is to certify that, I, Daw Aung San Suu Kyi agreed to the entry of the following person's name in the Family Card of my residence at No. 54/56 University Avenue, Bahan Township, Yangon.

U Myint Soe (12/Ah la na (n) 048010 (father) U Ohn Maung, No. 157, Nguwar Road, Hta Nar Yat Kwet, Ahlone Township.

Daw Aung San Suu Kyi

(This certificate was written by Daw Aung San Suu Kyi from Insein Prison to say that she agreed to the entry of my name in her family list card. It enabled me to gain legal access to her in prison but I thought it was a bad omen to use it, in case it lead to a longer stay actually happening. (Ama often had somebody enquire whether I had entered my name in her family list yet or not.) The letter of is still with me because now it belongs to history: it is a souvenir in memory of her 10 years of imprisonment from 1999 to 2009.)

"KMS will offer soon daw (the meritorious offering of a bowl of rice), the glasses of water, the candles and the flowers daily to Lord Buddha as usual. You will also do the daily sweeping and cleaning as usual, and feed the kittens as usual. Let the weekly sweepers and cleaners do their weekly duties as usual and give them their food as usual. Let me trust you will do as you are told. You two should behave yourselves while I am away."

Whenever she was leaving us alone to go to somewhere for some time, she always used to remind us to behave ourselves in her absence. Both of us were quite familiar with those words. We rarely behaved ourselves while she was away. If you asked us whether we were bad guys we would answer we were not so. We're each that sort of guy who is not so good and not so bad. (Oh, we've been around Ama nearly 23 years!)

When I stood downcast while listening to her words, she said, "KMS, don't stand that way. Raise your head, smile and assume a happy gait. Go and ask when the car is coming. When it arrives, put these suitcases in it. See me off in a joyful manner."

(May I ask you, my good friends, would you be able to assume a happy look in such a situation? Could you be detached and stayed without emotion in such a plight? Ama was unmoved and looked as if she were a superwoman who could face the vicissitudes of life with complete calmness of spirit.)

I went and asked when the car would arrive. The car arrived at 6:55am and left at 7am. I saw her off up to the threshold of the compound.

My diary for this historic day reads as follows:

May 14, 2009 (Thursday)

No outings were allowed the whole day. The police regimental commander told us that he requested this due to an order given by the police chief. They told us they will do the buying of meals for us (we had asked them to do this for us). In the evening the police commander's letter was read to us. Tomorrow we will be allowed to go out but no outsider will be allowed to come in. Whenever one of us goes out, the other has to stay inside.

I arrived at Ama's compound at 6am. I was allowed inside and met with her. She handed over the set of keys. She told Ko Ni and me to look after the house.

The list of daily provision was sent.

They took her at 7am. Ama was prosecuted at the special court in Insein Jail under articles 10(a), 10(b) and 22 of the law safeguarding the state from subversive elements.

I was quite familiar with Ama's house so there were no problems looking after the household duties. But one thing that gave me trouble was my ignorance of the *puja* mantra for offering a bowl of rice or a bouquet of flowers or some glasses of pure water to the Lord Buddha. I was not a stranger to religious ceremonies, but I was ignorant of said mantra and that gave me some trouble.

I woke up at 5am and listened to the Mandalay FM radio program on the history of great pagodas, presented in an interesting manner by broadcaster Ma Soe Ein Thu. Then I continued listening to songs and music for enjoyment. I did some jogging around my large square bedroom. After the music from Mandalay FM, I listened to the VOA, RFA and BBC short-wave broadcasts for daily news. Then I went upstairs to offer candles and incense sticks to the Lord Buddha. I made a *puja* of incense sticks to the spiritual beings who take responsibility for Ama's well-being and good fortune, just as I did every morning and night.

Then I cooked some rice to offer the morning *soon* (a plate of rice) to the Lord Buddha and for our morning meal. (Curries and dishes to go with our meals were taken care of by Ko Htay Aung's family and we had to go and fetch them every day.)

Afterward the kittens were fed. Next I took the brooms and shovel and started sweeping the altar room and then continued sweeping one room after another until all the rooms upstairs were free of dust. There being a great number of house lizards around, the house had to be swept clean of their droppings. I first thought of clearing them once every three days, but the amount was so large I had to do it every day.

At 10am I made preparations for the offering of *soon* to the Lord Buddha. Each day I sat and offered five glasses of water and paid respect to the Buddha and made a solemn vow to observe the *Pansa Sila* (five precepts). I offered the *soon* and sent metta (loving-kindness) to Ama and to all living beings. Then I chanted *dharana paritta and pattana paritta*. Thus it took nearly 15 minutes to do my religious duties. I have gained much merit lately because in my life before this I rarely sat before the Lord Buddha for such a long time. I thank Ama for the meritorious deeds I have done for her sake.

After my morning religious duties were done, I went to Ko Htay Aung's house to fetch the curry and dishes for us as usual. Whenever I went outside for this purpose, I also did anything else that needed to be done outside and visited whomever we needed to visit.

Ama had asked me to let the house cleaners, who did their job every Tuesday, continue as usual while she was away. So every Tuesday I arranged for their lunch at noon and for their afternoon meal at 3pm, with either coffee or cold drinks and cakes or biscuits. After their duties were done at 5pm, I let them take their baths and afterward gave them their wages in cash. These were the jobs I did only after my arrival at the house. Previously it had been Aunty Win's duty to give them breakfast and lunch. Now I had to give them breakfast and lunch myself, but that was the only difference. Another duty I had was to listen to the radio. I had to listen to news about Ama and about what was happening in the country because these things were important now.

In the meantime a strange thing happened. The *gangaw* (*mesua ferrea*) flowers in her compound had bloomed off-season during the rainy season, not those on the huge fifteen-foot trees but those from the one that was only three feet tall. I had to go out and enquire about the possible implications of such an omen. I was told it was an omen of good luck. So I offered the blossoms to the Lord Buddha (flowers were offered regularly every Tuesday and Saturday) and prayed for lucky things to happen. My subconscious was telling me that Ama would be coming back soon.

Ama had told us not to sleep downstairs together and for one of us to sleep upstairs while the other remained downstairs. So I told Ko Htay Aung to go upstairs and sleep there, because I was afraid to sleep there alone. The next night he refused to go there, saying he found it difficult to fall asleep because it was too hot there. Because the windows upstairs were locked up for security reasons, it was rather hot there. Neither of us slept there from then on, although we went up there at night to make a careful check.

May 28, 2009 (Thursday)

At 2pm Mr Yettaw, the American citizen who had involved Ama in a legal offence, arrived back again. This was the third time he had arrived here, but this time he came legally, with a full retinue. I was amazed. They had come to retrace his illegal entry route into Ama's compound, so I saw him close up. He led them around to this place and to that place. He got thirsty so I had to offer him some water. When I told him (through an acquaintance) not to involve me in a legal offence for offering him water, he smiled.

June 2009

In the meantime something happened concerning the ownership of Ama's house that meant we had to get legally involved. Nearly one month after Ama's custody in Insein jail began, probably around June, a classified ad for the sale of a land plot with Ama's house number appeared in a newspaper column. Although no street name was mentioned in the advertisement, on careful scrutiny it turned out to be Ama's house. The information had to be communicated immediately to Ama. It was due mainly to Ko Htay Aung's cleverness that we learned of the matter in good time. Otherwise it would have been too late. Ama had to consult with U Kyi Win and U Nyan Win and let them take action about this act of conspiracy against her.

July 3, 2009 (Friday)

I felt as if I was singing a song in my mind. The song was "*Yuzana* Tree and a Yellow Ribbon" which was sung some 40 years ago by Marshal, the husband of my friend Yamin. I think the original English song is "Tie a Yellow Ribbon (Round the Old Oak Tree)". I had forgotten the full words to the song, but I still remembered the tune. When I looked toward the gate of the compound I saw the *yuzana* tree there, so I hurried to Bogyoke Aung San Market and bought a reel of yellow ribbon. I cut many one-foot-long ribbons and tied each of them to the *yuzana* tree with the help of a stapler. I was given a helping hand with the job by Ko Htay Aung.

July 4, 2009 (Saturday)

I got up at 5am and tied the yellow ribbons on the upper trunks of all the *yuzana* trees at the head of the compound. One of the bows was tied on the top of the entrance gate also. That was the day in which

Ban Ki-moon paid a visit to Myanmar. His motorcade drove past our front gate at 5pm that evening. I stood in front of our front gate in a UN T-shirt and made a welcoming wave.

Third week of July, 2009

Every six months Ko Htay Aung had a medical checkup and the due date for his latest check had already passed. So he went to Dr Tin Myo Win in the third week of July. I was left alone in the compound. Aunty Ni and Munar came at 7am and left at noon. At night I was alone, so I could not sleep well because I was afraid (you see, I've got the blood of Maha Bandoola, the great Myanmar general, in me). So I sat up all night. The reason I sat up all night could also be attributed to security. In the whole compound there was only one person. It was rather historic, that situation which lasted nearly a fortnight. When Ama learned of the situation an additional companion was allowed in. Ama arranged for Maung Tint Lwin, who had been a previous resident here, to be my new companion. Only after that could I sleep at night. Aunty Ni, Munar and U Htin Kyaw also came every day.

August 11, 2009 (Tuesday)

By and by the first week of August arrived. It was only three days to go before the three months of Ama's arrest reached their duration. Today the final order would be handed down. As soon as daylight came I offered candles and five glasses of water to the Lord Buddha and sat respectfully and chanted eleven *paritta* sutras, *pattana desana* and *dharana paritta*. At 10am I offered soon and as I went downstairs afterward the doorbell rang. When I went to the gate compound to enquire, security officials told me firmly to stay inside the compound. So I thought something unusual might be happening. I looked toward the bows of yellow ribbon atop the *yuzana* trees, thinking about whether the things I had been thinking would materialise.

Just after 11:30am they called me and repeated their warning that I was not to go outside. So I felt very happy. My welcoming gesture of yellow ribbons on *yuzana* trees was right, I was quite sure. They told me to let Aunty Ni and party go home if they wished to do so. I asked

Aunty Ni to stay on and she asked me to seek permission to let her stay up until 1pm as usual. I went and told them about her request and they allowed it.

At noon a group of women arrived with pots of rice, curry dishes and crockery. They were the group that voluntarily catered Ama's meals at Insein jail each day. They told me that they came here to offer us meals because Ama wasn't taking meals yet. I told them that Ama was not yet here and that she was the only person who could say yes or no to their coming inside, as I did not have the authority. I let them see Aunty Ni because they wanted to see her. Aunty Ni told them that Ama had entrusted me and my companion with the affairs of her house and compound, and that they came just to give a helping hand. The most responsible person was KMS, she said. She asked them to wait until Ama's arrival. She told them that if Ama agreed to their request, nobody could refuse.

At 12:45pm they asked for the front gate to be opened because Ama's motorcade was approaching Inya Road. So I opened the front gate and looked toward Inya Road in expectation.

Not long afterward the motorcade arrived at the front gate and the first four cars drove into the compound while the remaining cars stopped along the road. Ama was in one of the four cars while Aunty Daw Khin Win and her daughter were in another one. Ama said thanks to the people who came along and also to the woman doctor who came along. She expressed happiness at seeing U Moe Hein, Aunty Ni and brother U Htin Kyaw. While asking about the visit of the house repairmen she told Aunty Ni, "Ma Ni, the house needs to be repaired but I haven't got the cash for it. You will have to pay for the repairs yourself." Aunty Ni replied, "Don't you worry about that, Aunty. I will surely take care of that." On hearing their conversation I felt sorry for Ama's lack of means, even when it came to the upkeep of her house. When Ama asked whether the idea of yellow ribbons on the *yuzana* trees was mine, I just smiled.

Since Ama hadn't had her meal yet, she asked me to buy "whatever you think is best". U Moe Hein and I hastened to Kyetshazun restaurant on Goodlife Road and bought three packages of biryani for her.

After 2pm security officials came and told us to let Aunty Ni and party go home, and so they went back home. Ama asked the security gate authorities to allow me to stay at her home 24 hours a day. The security authorities replied that they would have to seek approval from Pyinmana and asked her to wait until 4pm for a reply. I was compelled to wait there with her until that time. At 4pm a reply came saying that I was not allowed to stay overnight. I could buy and bring in necessary food and could enter the compound at 9am to cook and serve meals for Ama, but I had to go back at 5pm. Ama gave her consent.

"Every morning you will buy food for me and cook it," she said. "Daw Khin Khin Win and her daughter will cook their own meals for themselves, but you should bring back whatever they want. After cooking the evening meals you can go back home. You will have to be mindful of the times they have set for you."

She added that we must be rather thankful that they allowed my entrance, given previous curtailments they had imposed. Previously I had to leave immediately after the food was sent into the compound in the morning. Now that I was allowed to go inside to cook the meals and serve her, it became more convenient for her. No matter what, Ama is our top priority.

I bought whatever Ama wanted me to buy. At 9am I entered the compound and prepared her breakfast. For her I needn't cook things early. I started cooking at about 11am and she usually had her lunch at 12pm. (She told me beforehand what time she would have her lunch.)

Aunty Ni and party were not allowed to enter anymore. (She had been managing Ama's affairs at her best she could from 1995 up until that day.) After a week's time, I was not allowed inside either. The security people allowed me to bring whatever Ama had asked for up to the threshold of the gate. Ama knew that it was rather inconvenient for me, but it couldn't be helped. We all had to do what we could to support her. So I couldn't enter the gates at 9am as usual. I could do so only after 10am. I therefore had to take a taxi to reach the compound, not a bus as before. Previously I was given K1000 for travelling expenses, but it didn't cover my trips in a taxi, so I had to ask for more travelling expenses. The meals had to be carried to the house after being cooked outside, so it was time-consuming.

I sent her meals from outside in a taxi everyday. By then, some of the yellow ribbons were still left on the *yuzana* trees although some of them had fallen to the ground because of the wind. The ribbons made me smile when I realised the truth inherent in the song. Tying a yellow ribbon on a tree trunk may help bring back somebody you have been expecting. I carried on gently singing "Tie a Yellow Ribbon" to myself.

(In remembrance of August 2009)

—*The Myanmar Times (Vol. 30, No. 596-597, 2012)*

A memory of my encounters with our sister

I relish the study of historical biographies and events. For instance, the early stories of the 1962 Revolutionary Council and Thakin Tin Mya's writings about the Burmese Socialist Program Party are things to be remembered. What *yebaw* Ba Khet wrote about the BCP (Burma Communist Party) and their experiences when they went underground in the forest are records of real historical events. Because of them, history cannot be forgotten or destroyed.

At 5pm on July 20, 1989, the order that confined Ama to house arrest under Article 10(b) of the law safeguarding the state from the dangers of subversive elements was served. The rest of us were sent to Insein jail under Article 10(a) of the same law.

Article 10(a) of the law sentenced the accused to jail while Article 10(b) of the law sentenced him or her to house arrest. Under both articles the accused had to be remanded every six months and he or she could be detained up to six months. In 1991, the three-year term of imprisonment was changed into a six-year term of imprisonment.

Because Ama had already served two years when the term of imprisonment was changed to five years she had to remain under house arrest for three more years. She was set to finish five years of house arrest on July 20, 1994, but she was freed on July 10, 1995, at 6pm.

On the morning of July 11 a huge crowd of people (guests who wanted to see her and reporters from the journals) gathered in front of the main gate. The reporters were allowed in to see her in groups and she went in front of her compound to give a speech to the public. She gave welcoming speeches to the public every evening. She developed an understanding with them and saw them every Saturday and Sunday from 4pm to 5pm, first making a speech and afterward holding a question-and-answer session. The crowds became larger and larger.

A large vacant space in front of her house had been turned into a thatch-roofed hall and important events and speeches were held there. Celebrations for Independence Day, Union Day, Revolution Day, Thingyan Festival, General Election Anniversary Day, Ama's birthday, the NLD anniversary and National Day were held there.

At the May 1996 celebration for the General Elections Anniversary, things took a different turn. Ko Ko Nyi (U Aye Win) and Ko Htein (U Win Htein) were taken away and a group of delegations from the states and divisions were enclosed inside the compound. (They were: Dr Than Nyein of Yangon Division; U Tin Chaw, U Mann Johny, Dr Myo Nyunt, Dr Tin Min Htut and David Hla Myint of Ayeyarwady Division; U Aye and U Thar Maung from Bago; U Chit Tin and U Soe Myint from Magwe; and U Aung Kyi Nyunt of Mon State.)

The roads were closed and nobody could go out. Only I was allowed to go out to buy food. I went out with the blue Sunny pickup Da/3006 for the purpose and was interrogated at every security gate.

November 9, 1996 (Saturday)

Although the usual Saturday- and Sunday-evening meetings with the public were closed, the public and NLD members continued to come as usual, though they were allowed only as far as the eastern end of Kokkine Road. When Ama tried to go out and meet them she encountered opposition. Later the public was allowed to proceed up to U Chit Maung Road and Goodlife Road only. Our sister went and met them. She left her compound at 3pm in her own car, with the Sunny pickup and U Tin Oo's car following closely behind and two security cars following suit. Some delegates and youths from her compound were inside the Sunny pickup. The motorcade drove up to U Kyi Maung's home where he was picked up by U Tin Oo's car. Ama asked me to ride along with the two elderly people to keep them company.

On leaving U Kyi Maung's home the Sunny pickup took the lead position in front of Ama's car and U Tin Oo's car. The security officer's blue van followed the motorcade closely and the police security car followed from the rear. When the motorcade drove past Kanbawza Avenue and turned right onto Kaba Aye Pagoda Road and pulled up in front of the No. 121 and No. 123 compounds, a crowd of nearly 300 people had blocked the road ahead and asked the cars to stop. The leading Sunny pickup escaped while the mob attacked our cars with sticks, steel chains and bricks. The windscreens of U Tin Oo's car and the security officer's car were broken. Only when an officer from the security car ordered the mob to stop at gunpoint did they stop fighting. We had to drive off in a hurry.

When the motorcade reached Bosein Hman Street it turned left onto U Chit Maung Road and finally arrived at Goodlife Road where the public was waiting for Ama. The public, on seeing the condition of our cars, came closer and asked anxiously about our unfortunate encounters, but Ama made her public address without fail. On our return trip we drove northward along Kaba Aye Pagoda Road up to the traffic lights and turned left and drove along the Parami Road up to AD Road. From there we turned left and drove along Pyay Road. Then we turned onto Inya Road and finally turned onto University Avenue. When we came close to Inya Myaing Road we saw the road ahead was being blocked by nearly 300 people. So we stopped our cars at the entrance to Thanlwin (Windermere) Road.

Ama asked me to go and consult with security officer Ko Thuya. Even security officer Ko Thuya's car was being attacked. He said he could no longer take responsibility for us for the time being and he advised Ama to rest somewhere until he received further security measures for us from higher authorities. Ama sent me again to ask Ko Thuya whether we would be allowed to go to U Tin Oo's home, which was the only place we could go to. Ko Thuya agreed, saying, "Go ahead. We are coming along too." So Ama told the cars to drive onto

Thanlwin Road. As we drove onto the road a man was seen following our cars with a dagger in his hand. The security police car shooed him away and he was seen hastening into an old office building.

We all drove along Thanlwin Road and finally reached U Tin Oo's home on Aung Min Gaung Road, where we took some rest and recounted our experiences. At 7pm Ko Thuya wanted to see us and Ama sent me to see him. Kò Thuya asked me to tell Ama that we could go back home now, and that one of their cars would lead the way and our cars were to follow behind. His motorcade would also follow. With one of Ko Thuya's cars leading us we proceeded along Inya Road, Dhamaseti Road and Shwetaungyar Road. We entered University Avenue from the side of Aung Zeya Road and finally entered Ama's compound. Only then could we feel relieved.

Such suspenseful events took place often in our lives. This was only one of the many events that we passed through too often. Let me commit a wanton vandalism into remembrance.

— *The Myanmar Times (Vol. 30, No. 599, 2012)*

Because of wearing a T-shirt with Ama's portrait

When I saw Ama again in 2010 after her release, the situation had changed a lot. The tense situations had relaxed. Many people had become courageous. Those who had not dared to be friendly with her previously had become friendly. A couple of businesspeople became daring enough to sell photographs and T-shirts bearing her portraits. (I was happy to see people wearing T-shirts with Ama's portrait or with her father's portrait. I am a dogmatic admirer of Aung San.)

Journals could not put Ama's photographs on their pages yet. News of her could be printed but not photographs. Journals that ventured to show Ama's photographs were ordered to stop publication for one or two weeks. (They were so fearful of Ama's popularity. Think how fearful they would be of Ama in person.)

After August 19, 2010, when Ama's father's portrait appeared at the presidential residence, the journals that printed Aung San's photograph or photographs of Ama sold like hotcakes. The rare photographs of her father and herself reappeared in profusion.

In April 2012, when it became known that our sister had chosen to contest a seat in parliament in the by-elections, representations of national symbols – her father's photographs, T-shirts with her portraits, NLD memorabilia, pinny jackets and *yaw htamis* (sarongs)

– flooded the length and breadth of Myanmar. It reminded me of the 1990 general elections. On November 14, 2010, the day after our sister was freed, roadside stalls and hawkers along Shwegondaing Road, New Yedarshay Road and Old Yedarshay Road that led to the Shwegondaing NLD headquarters did very good business, selling out all their beverages and food-stuffs. They were left wishing every day could be as good as that day.

Previously when I sported a T-shirt with Ama's portrait, people around Shwegondaing Junction stared at me. When I asked a fabric printer friend of mine at Shwegondaing Junction to print me a number of T-shirts with Ama's portrait, they replied that they dared not do it. They said they were doing the print works and green flags of the USDP party. Now the greens have disappeared and the red-and-yellow flags and portraits of Ama have taken their place. Times have changed so fast.

When everybody dared to start wearing T-shirts with her portrait, acquaintances wearing those shirts teased me. "You're not the only one who wears that shirt," they would say. "You see, we're all wearing that!" I had been wearing those T-shirts since 1989. Those I wore then were printed abroad. Later, friends gave me more as presents.

In those days, when people saw me wearing T-shirts bearing Aung San Suu Kyi's portrait, some asked me whether I was afraid of being arrested. Others asked where I bought them. Some said, "Bravo!" I did not care what people said. I just acted according to my own beliefs.

When I spoke the truth some people didn't relish it. Even the guys who had been together with me during imprisonment and who went together to pay respect to Ama when she was freed in 1995 were different. While I stayed on in her compound, they left. Some of them did business for a living. One of them invited me to pay visits to his home, to keep him informed of Ama's news. So I went to his home once every fortnight. By 1996, however, the situation had changed somewhat. There were curtailments to her movements. After these changes he started to show a cold shoulder to me on my visits. When I failed to recognise his signs he told me he would like me to stop coming. Later I learned that he had been awarded construction contracts from a government ministry, so he didn't want to have much to do with us.

One fabric printer told me not to come in wearing a T-shirt with

The author wearing T-shirt with Daw Aung San Suu Kyi's portrait was interrogated by authorities on September 21, 1998.

Daw Suu's portrait because some authorities also paid business visits to his place. I had to wear an ordinary dress shirt to cover up my T-shirt. After 2010, however, his business made huge profits from selling Daw Suu T-shirts. In six months' time he made millions and became a rich man.

In fact, they were right to be worried. Maybe they were worried because they'd heard the story of me being taken in for interrogation because I was wearing a T-shirt with Daw Suu's portrait on it.

The story was: On September 21, 1998, when Ama was on a little bridge near Kyizu Village on the Hlaingtharyar-Nyaungdone motorway, we stayed behind at her house as watchmen. Dr Tin Myo Win and Ma Pyone were allowed to follow her for her daily health checkup. Dr Tin Myo Win was coming at 11am to take back things I had bought for Ama. I wanted to give him a bottle of orange juice for her. I went to City Mart at Aung San Stadium to buy one, wearing a T-shirt with Daw Suu's portrait as usual. While I was waiting for a bus at the Hpasapala bus stand, three men came forward and stood on my left, another three on my right and five behind me. A little later a man came face-to-face with me and told me to follow him. All of them surrounded me. When I asked him why, he replied that he had something to ask me and led me to what looked to be an office in the Hpasapala complex. Once inside the room they asked me to sit on a stool. Later, the township SLORC chairman and a township officer arrived and interrogated me.

"What do you come here for? Where do you live? Where are you going?" When I answered them they become wide-eyed and started taking notes in their small notebooks. Afterward they all left the room and left me alone. A water bottle was offered to me and they asked me whether I would like to chew betel-quid. Everything seemed quiet. A bit later a small group of cars stopped in front of the office. When the people inside the cars alighted they turned out to be officers from No. 4 Area Command, Yangon. The officer in charge spoke into a phone. "Yes, G-1, I've just arrived. We learned from his statements that he had been buying something for Daw Suu. I will interrogate him for myself, sir." He came close to me and asked me to stand up, saying he wanted to look at my shirt, then he reported back through the phone. "He wears a T-shirt with a red Daw Suu sticker with the words 'I am not afraid' below it. He also wears a hat and he wears a foreign-made badge on his lapel."

When he asked me whether he could take my T-shirt as evidence, I told him, "I cannot give this shirt away. You can arrest me if you want, but not this shirt. I will apply for a licence to wear this shirt if you can issue me one." I didn't understand what the other side was saying through the phone. Later, he told me, "Please sit for a while. Daw Suu will be home soon. Today is the last day the NLD asked to be allowed to call parliamentary meetings. This happened because we are watching carefully for security breaches everywhere. As you happen to be wearing a Daw Suu T-shirt, all of us were keeping an eye on you. That's why this interrogation happened."

I replied, "I usually buy things for Daw Suu at City Mart. I don't know what NLD has demanded or what statements it has issued. My only duty is to prepare meals for her. I came here to buy things for her."

He told me, "We'll send you back," but I thanked him for saying so and asked him to allow me to go back on my own. He warned me that I could encounter the same sort of interrogation again and advised me to change my T-shirt for an ordinary shirt. I told him that I hadn't got any spare shirt and that I would wear the T-shirt inside-out. So saying, I took off the T-shirt, turned it inside-out and wore it in that fashion. One of them said he had a spare shirt and offered to let me wear it, but I refused.

As I left the office, I saw a huge crowd waiting outside. The news seemed to have been communicated through word of mouth that a person wearing a T-shirt with Daw Suu's portrait had been arrested. In Hpasapala Ward there was one family in particular that had warm relations with Daw Suu. They must have thought that the one who had been arrested for wearing a Daw Suu T-shirt must be none other than me. They were certainly right in their thinking. People in Hpasapala Ward who knew me were also watching from the crowd. The authorities saw me off up to the time I got on the bus.

When Ama was told about the City Mart incident, her response was, "KMS will always be like that."

(I contented myself with the thought that, because of the plights I had often fallen into, people might not be so afraid anymore of being thought of as an accomplice.)

Here I would like to relate something that Ama told me once. It was a revelation of her inner feeling. It was in 1999. When we were deep in conversation she told me, "I am very sorry that they have been trying to obliterate the role my father played in history." I replied to her, "Ama, whatever those who wish to obliterate may do, your father is the historic national leader. They're the ones who will be obliterated. They will be powerful as long as their power lasts – not beyond that."

It doesn't take long. Everybody has seen how the life of the person who says "there shall never be democracy in my division, in my place" will come to an end. How the one who said, in Indonesia, "Aung San Suu Kyi is like a little ant, a little vermin, and if swept by a broom she will be gone" was himself swept away like a vermin. If you look at things in a religious way, fearful lessons will be learned. (What you sow, so will you reap – even in your lifetime.)

Not very long after our discussion about her father, T-shirts with her father's portrait and the words "Tatmadaw begins with Aung San" flooded the T-shirt market. I wore the T-shirt with greatest of happiness.

Since the portrait of Ama's father first reappeared in the guest room of the president's office on August 19, 2011, it could be seen almost everywhere in Myanmar. I believe Ama must have felt happiness engulfing her whole being.

Now that everybody has been wearing Bogyoke and Daw Suu T-shirts, I have kept away from wearing them myself. Some people ask me cynically, "Why don't you wear them now? Are you afraid of being arrested?" I reply to them, "I never wear them when everybody dares to wear them; I wear them only when nobody dares to wear them!"

– Open News (Vol. 5, No. 11, December 2012)

A Thai girl who loves and respects Daw Aung San Suu Kyi

Shortly after Daw Aung San Suu Kyi arrived back from Thailand, when she was making the rounds of her first European tour, a Thai girl and her friend arrived in Myanmar. Her aim was to study Myanmar, and her main focus was learning about and seeing Daw Suu.

She didn't know much about Daw Suu's European tour. She thought Daw Suu was still in Myanmar. We came across each other by a lucky chance. I like those who love and respect Ama very much. On haphazard study, she looked like one who is crazy about Ama. I stay aloof with most people: I keep away from foreigners, diplomats and reporters. Because she was crazy about Ama like me, though, I welcomed her very warmly. (I never deal with people in such a warm manner otherwise.)

She was a Thai youth of over 20 years of age. She was only two years old in 1988 when Ama entered into politics. From 1995 to 1996, when news of Daw Aung San Suu Kyi started making headlines in the international media, she was only about 9 years old and she knew nothing about Daw Suu. Only in 2010, when news of Ama flooded world headlines, did she begin to take interest in them. She wondered who Daw Aung San Suu Kyi was. So she studied her avidly. She started to learn some things about Ama's father. She learned that Bogyoke Aung San was the national leader of Myanmar; that he was the father of the Myanmar Tatmadaw; that he was one of the thirty comrades who, while in Bangkok, had sliced their arms and collected their combined blood in a silver bowl and drank it with a vow to form the Myanmar army; and that Ama is the daughter of Myanmar's national leader. So she studied Ama's life and became crazy about her like myself.

When she read the news in the Thai and international media of Daw Suu's planned first visit to Thailand, to deliver a speech at the Economic Forum, she wanted to see Ama and studied her schedule carefully. She went to the airport to see her in person and took pictures of her. When she learned of Ama's planned visit to Mahar Chaing to see the Myanmar workers there, she sought help from her friend to accompany her there and her friend fulfilled the request. There were more than 100,000 Myanmar workers. Daw Suu gave a speech from the third floor of the Mahar Chaing workers' building. The girl recorded Ama making a speech with her camera. She also took snapshots of Daw Aung San Suu Kyi getting out of and into her car.

She had tried to get a closer view of Ama and she had succeeded in doing so. She was quite pleased. Daw Suu's speech was in the Myanmar language and she didn't understand the words, but she was convinced that Daw Aung San Suu Kyi is a leader and she was crazy about her for that.

She had seen Daw Suu only fleetingly in Thailand, though, so she was not yet satisfied. She wanted to see more of her. So she and her friend made plans to pay a visit to Myanmar. They did come and they met me on Ama's birthday, a day to be remembered. The birthday celebration happened in the morning and they came in the evening, after the NLD office was closed. They don't know it was Daw Suu's birthday. After meeting with me they asked questions in a foreign language I found hard to understand. Here in Myanmar we are used to communicating with foreign visitors through an interpreter. I have never seen anyone talking directly without a go-between (I have only seen Daw Aung San Suu Kyi speaking directly without an intermediary). I communicated with them through body language.

She is not an ordinary person. She had listened to the speeches made by Ama at Mahar Chaing; she showed me the photos of Ama she had taken with her camera, as well as photos taken at Bogyoke's museum on Tower Lane. She also talked about Daw Aung San Suu Kyi's family, that there were three siblings. On a piece of paper she wrote down the date Daw Suu's brother Ko Ko Lin (Ko Aung San Lin)

Daw Aung San Suu Kyi's Thai visit (2012)

drowned. She also told me Daw Suu's father's birthday. I could not help respecting her. I became friendly with her. She said that she wanted to buy some commemorative Daw Aung San Suu Kyi souvenirs and asked me where to get them. I told her to come to the office the next day. They said they were returning to Thailand tomorrow evening and that they would come for the things they needed before that. Then they said goodbye to me.

The next afternoon they came to the office to buy things. They asked my friend about me by describing my features. My friend came and called me. As I remembered them, I helped them. They were very friendly toward me. I gave them souvenirs of Daw Aung San Suu Kyi as presents. They accepted the presents heartily and we sat down and talked. She then asked me questions. "Is there anyone other than Daw Aung San Suu Kyi who is loved by the Myanmar people? Are there deputy leaders?" I told her that Daw Suu was the only one and there were no others. She said that there was no leader like her in her own country and that only King Bhumibol was respected and revered by the Thais. She became tearful when saying that when the king passes away there will be no leader to respect and revere.

I replied that I respected their king and that I knew that her king loved the Thai people like his own children. When I told her about the king she became respectful toward me.

I also dwelt on their country's history, the relationship between our two countries, admonitions against and imitations of Thai culture here, the eras when different Thai generals governed Thailand and the strong bonds that existed between the two countries and how proud I was of them.

Daw Aung San Suu Kyi's Thai visit (2012)

I also told them that I was grateful to the Thai king and the Thai people for giving assistance to democratic forces and for helping the refugees in the border areas for many years. These acts deserve thanks. I also thanked them for giving jobs to the unemployed people and immigrants. (There might be negligible problems but they are not inexcusable.)

I told them about the visit (in the company of an ASEAN women's delegation) of a relative of the Thai king to Daw Aung San Suu Kyi. I told them that I could still visualise the moment when they gave a basket of orchids to Daw Suu as a birthday present.

I related to her some bits and pieces that I remembered and we exchanged names and addresses. She asked me to give a card to Daw Suu and in return I gave her a T-shirt, photo and key chain with Daw Aung San Suu Kyi's pictures on them as presents. Her name card shows:

Ms. Narintip Thongsaichon (Pook)
The Stock Exchange of Thailand
62 Rathapisek Road
Klongtoey, Bangkok 10110
Thailand.

The first foreign trip for Ama in 20 years was to Thailand. Naturally the Thai people are intrigued. I am full of thanks to the Thai government and people for giving top coverage of the trip and also to the Thai security teams, included the female officers. When Daw Aung San Suu Kyi was freed from house arrest in November 2010, the world's media, including the Thai media, came here to cover the news. When it was broadcast back in Thailand, the Thai people came to know more about Daw Aung San Suu Kyi. Once there was transparency, Thai youths felt the urge to know more about her. In their country there is no such thing as a people's leader but only party leaders. At present, they have their country's first female prime minister which makes things more interesting for them. A Thai politician remarked that if he were to compete with Daw Aung San Suu Kyi, he would not win. The attitudes of my Thai visitor and my own are the same on this matter. That must be the reason she took a liking to me. Quite recently, I received a letter and presents from her. I was surprised. It must have been be a response to my goodwill, but I felt embarrassed. I must give her something back. She really adores Daw Aung San Suu Kyi.

(In remembrance of the lovely Thai girl Baby Pook)

– Open News (Vol. 4, No. 40, July 2012)

The lady in Myanmar attire whom the world has come to know

Not long ago we saw a Myanmar lady in her native attire who made speeches in prominent places in front of foreign dignitaries and whose words were broadcast on television around the world. She was invited by foreign dignitaries as their official guest. Out of Myanmar's population of 60 million people, 59 million took pride in this. That lady is a leader of one party in Myanmar's multi-party democracy era, and she is also a representative of the people's hluttaw.

This lady is not an ordinary Myanmar lady. She is a lady of many distinctions. Like her father, she has sacrificed herself without personal benefit in order to serve as a pioneer for democracy. For twenty years she sacrificed her family affairs and she was awarded the Nobel Peace Prize and other honours and distinctions from many countries. One can safely say that no other female has been showered with so many honours and prizes.

It is said that "the hand that rocks the cradle rules the world". We must accept that this Myanmar lady practises this saying. Too often we have only seen instances in which the hands that rock the cradle are used to spray pesticides and grow trees.

The rule of law will only prevail when people use the law and abide

Daw Aung San Suu Kyi in Myanmar attire

by it. We must be imbued with patriotism. If a Myanmar becomes distinguished and famous one must take pride in him or her and bestow honour upon that person. The Shan people took pride when Sai Aung Hlaing Myint was awarded the Henry Dunant prize. The same goes for Dr Cynthia Maung of the Mae Tao Clinic. The Kayins, naturally, were proud of her.

There was even a famous British soldier who fell in love with Burma. He was General Mountbatten. He acted as Commander-in-Chief of the Southeast Asia region during WWII, during which he was in charge of the Myanmar theatre of war, and also as served as Viceroy in India. He respected the Myanmar customs and mindset. He loved Burma and its people. When he signed his signature at the end of his letters, he always signed "Mountbatten of Burma". He was the one who ceremoniously returned to Myanmar the Thihathana throne used by the last Myanmar kings.

Myanmar women's attire is very famous because of the Lady (Daw Suu) who has worn Myanmar attire since childhood. After Ama's father's death, she was brought up by her mother who was a distinguished person in her own right. Theirs was a conservative family and Ama continues to wear Myanmar attire. She also has a penchant for wearing flowers in her hair. She shows her patriotism not only in words and deeds but also in her features.

Some time ago there was cartoon in a journal. It depicted a conversation between a Myanmar citizen and a tourist.

The Myanmar citizen is asking, "Do you know about teak and oil?"

The tourist replies, "I know about them from your media."

"Do you know about our gas and gems?"

"I know about them from your media."

"Do you know about our gifted and decent people?"

"I know about them from our media."

I like that cartoon. It shows, in a way, the lack of transparency in our country. The people's hluttaw chairman exhorts frankness and has said that no one is above the law. Writer Ye Yint Tint Swe has

Daw Aung San Suu Kyi together with Prince Charles and Camilla in London (2012)

said that the press scrutiny policy should not exist anymore. These actions show the essence of democracy. Leaving aside the men for a moment, however, are there no women's organisations that represent Myanmar women?

Daw Suu's esteemed status as the only Myanmar lady to have been bestowed with so many awards, prizes and honours around the world – shouldn't this be given the praise it deserves? I would like to ask Than Thar Win, Chit Thu Wai, She and Tun Eindra Bo to again sing the song "Women come forward" for the distinguished ladies such as Cynthia Maung, Naw May Oo, and Naw Susanna Hla Hla Soe who follow behind the Lady.

– Open News (Vol. 4, No. 42, July 2012)

Dear daughter Shwewar Yaung, I must tell you about a speech at Oxford University

Dear daughter,

You must be attending university. I wonder which university. I would like to know. You must be attending a university your parents can afford.

These days, parents who have foresight and can afford it send their children to good schools. There are opportunities to send their children to good schools. (Mother's Own Schools have also emerged. These schools get support from former premiers and ministers from Europe. It is really surprising.)

During *Ba Ba*'s schooldays there were many good schools such as the Methodist English High School, St Mary's etc. As for *Ba Ba*, I attended Saya Saw's school supervised by Theikpan Maung Wa, a famous author.

During my grandparents' time, people were sent to England for further studies. Most had ambitions of becoming barristers. There were many ICS (Indian Civil Service) people.

During my time there was progress in the education sector. Yangon and Mandalay universities were up to par with other universities from abroad. When the *Pyi* (socialist) era arrived, Myanmar's education standard declined. A group of advisors were assigned to support the education system but the country was not developed. The advisors thought that it would never be successful with the government people in charge and they brought in their people and tried to influence the management of the education ministry. Then private schools became state high schools and Yangon University was renamed Rangoon Arts and Science University (RASU). They also established a Natural Science University. The curriculum was changed many times from one year to the next. The matriculation exam results were divided into the "A" list and the "B" list.

Colleges, called Regional Colleges (RC), were established. RC-1 was situated in Bohtataung township, RC-2 in Hlaing township and RC-3 in Kyimyidine township. Later the advisors and some ministerial officials

Daw Aung San Suu Kyi at Oxford University after accepting
Honorary Doctorate of Law Degree

were sacked as there was no progress in the country during that time.

I read an article in a journal issued on Wednesday which said that during the socialist era an advisor and his friend met in their native town and the friend said, "What advice have you given to the government? It has been very difficult for us to implement." The adviser replied, "My friend, you don't understand. I have advised them that they cannot reverse their way." Then they both laughed.

Old students enjoyed their schooldays at Yangon University with its beautiful shady trees. It is pitiful to see university or college students attending schools located far away in the paddy fields, with only Malaysia *padauk* and ball-sky trees around.

In the old days, one became a teacher at a university only when over 30 or 40 years of age. Now one becomes an assistant lecturer at age 23, a lecturer at age 25 and a professor after 40. I thought the country's education system had progressed. There was one instance in which a senior assistant teacher welcomed a new school principal to her school. To her chagrin, she saw that the new school principal had once been her pupil.

Using all kinds of methods, cronies occupy land in Yangon. Only the plot of land from the Inya Lake embankment to the Hanthawaddy roundabout remains as it is. An economist who knows about this said that Yangon University campus should be well kept and maintained because, in other countries, universities stand as a proud tradition. Once, Yangon University stood in high esteem in Asia. Now people who have not even seen pictures of Oxford, Cambridge, Harvard, Yale or Bucknell universities try to make a laughing stock out of it. We must show understanding to the people.

Whatever they say, the new transparency has widened the knowledge of young people and also changed their outlook. It is heartening to know that these young people have a chance to choose their own ways to better their future. The IT era quickens the pace of people's lives. Conservatives traditionally want to look back. If they do they will be left behind.

The private education system was allowed to operate tuition classes in the past but now there are more schools. In the past people wished to send their children to diplomatic school or international school. Now there are Teacher Nilar School, ILBC, MLA, ES4E, TOTAL and NIEC, to name but a few.

When *Ba Ba* was young there were some embassies which had their own school for children of embassy personnel. The school operated by the Indonesian Embassy even accepts Myanmar children. You can see how much they emulate the international education system.

Now, let us look at our education system. The other day I heard that there would be a reduction in the state-owned sector and an increase in the private sector which will be taking on more responsibilities in the education and health sectors. We must be watchful that the education and health sectors do not fall into the hands of cronies. Education and health sectors are the most important sectors of the country. Students and patients should not become like mice to be experimented in a laboratory.

Now that I am talking about education to my dear daughter, I would like to mention a speech given by the distinguished lady Daw Suu when she was conferred an honorary Doctorate of Law degree by Oxford University.

In her speech, she spoke about her life at Oxford University, the years she spent as a mother and wife in the Park Town district, and how Oxford University stood by her during the years when she was under house arrest. She mentioned how she pulled herself together during her difficult years by remembering the time she spent at Oxford. When she saw the Oxford University students again she could visualise her happy student days when she was free from worries. She said the most important thing she learned at Oxford University was that it was not reading thick books that mattered but getting to know and respect the qualities of a cultivated society.

The best of a cultivated society does not come from Oxford University alone. Likewise, it does not exist only in Myanmar. It comes from all parts of the world. Her experience prepared her to face the not-so-good parts of society. What made her sad was that Myanmar university students have missed out on campus life for decades. Campus life makes it possible for one to mould one's life according to one's wishes. The youth of Myanmar have been missing

Daw Aung San Suu Kyi accepts honorary doctorate of Law from Oxford University in 2012.

out on having the freedom to chart their own-path. The Lady said she wished to see the lives of Myanmar's university students improve and develop, and that she would be very grateful if Oxford University would give assistance to that end.

In conclusion, she said, she owed her thanks to Oxford University which treated her as one of its children and prepared her to face the difficulties ahead with vigour.

This will serve as knowledge for you, my daughter.

– Open News (Vol. 4, No. 37, July 2012)

Gandhi and Nehru were influential in Ama's political vision and political life respectively

The Mizzima (Middle) region in India is a sacred area for Buddhists. It is part of the Indian sub-continent where India, Pakistan and Nepal are situated. Gautama (the Enlightened One) was a native of Nepal. Bodagaya and Lumbini are sacred places for Buddhists. You can even call India one of your relatives.

The historical facts of India and Myanmar are similar. India has become a British colony first, followed by Myanmar. Burma's last king, King Thibaw, was sent to India and died there, just as India's last king, King Zavershia, was sent to Burma and died here. The national movements in the struggle for freedom from the British colonialists were similar in both countries also, with communication between the two organisations. There was also unity between the two national leaders. Indian leader Jawaharlal Nehru and General Aung San were very close personally. India gained independence a year earlier than Myanmar did.

I have heard Daw Suu's speech made in New Delhi, India, on the evening of November 14, 2012, commemorating the 123rd anniversary of the birth of Indian leader Jawaharlal Nehru. I support the speech.

The people know Daw Aung San Suu Kyi follows Gandhi's path and way of thinking, though actually Jawaharlal Nehru and his family were more intimate with Daw Aung San Suu Kyi. Daw Aung San Suu Kyi used to receive postcards from Sonia Gandhi through the Indian Embassy. (At that time Sonia had not yet entered politics.) After 1996, maybe because of the changing times, the postcards stopped coming.

During the struggle for democracy in 1988, India gave support in the initial stages. Afterward, it was not so supportive. When the opposition Janata Party gained power it became more distant. Even after the Congress Party regained power, only some voiced support for the democracy struggle. It was disheartening when the Indian government did not support the movement. There was one thing we were grateful for, however, and that was that it gave asylum to democratic forces.

By 2012, one could say there had been some slight changes in the outlook of the Indian government. When the prime minister of India, Manmohan Singh, visited Myanmar in June 2012, a formal invitation from Sonia Gandhi, then the ruling Congress Party chairperson, was conveyed to Daw Aung San Suu Kyi.

On November 13, 2012, Daw Aung San Suu Kyi paid a goodwill

Indian leader Mahatama Gandhi and Jawaharlal Nehru

visit to India. The Indian Foreign Minister personally welcomed her at the airport. Meeting the Indian vice president, the prime minister and Sonia Gandhi made Daw Aung San Suu Kyi seem like a national leader.

Daw Aung San Suu Kyi and Sonia Gandhi's meeting rekindled memories of the Nehru and Aung San families. Mahatma Gandhi's political thinking influenced Daw Aung San Suu Kyi during her younger days, but when she entered political life, Jawaharlal's views influenced her. The relationship which started with the long coat is still treasured. It has endured 65 years.

In 1995, Daw Aung San Suu Kyi was awarded the Jawaharlal Nehru Prize. Daw Than Aye and Lady Gore-Booth received the prize on her behalf at Nehru Hall on November 14, Nehru's birthday. At the prize-giving ceremony Daw Aung San Suu Kyi gave an address by video link.

At present, we see that Indo-Myanmar relations as well as world-Myanmar relations are changing. The world has begun to acknowledge Myanmar's reform and there is no denying that credit must be given to President U Thein Sein and to Daw Aung San Suu Kyi. Her role should be acknowledged. We must value and respect people who work for the country's benefit. There is evidence that she is not an ordinary person.

Ganges and Ayeyarwaddy, Chindwin and Yamona, flow together and let us build a long-term relationship between India and Myanmar.

– Open News (Vol. 5, No. 8, November 2012)

"National Spirit" and "Flaming Torch of Independence" music tapes

About 21 years ago, two songs, "National Spirit" and "Flaming Torch of Independence", were sung by singer Khin Nyunt Yee. They were produced by the Tekkatho Recording Studio. On each tape, there were two songs concerning Bogyoke Aung San. During that time I was released from Insein Prison. Those who wanted to omit Bogyoke Aung San's role from history banned anything that contained his name. When I overheard the song with Bogyoke Aung San's name in it, I was surprised that it had been produced legally. It is not wrong to say that it had been produced in remembrance of the 1990 elections. I bought those two tapes and listened to the songs almost daily. Even when Daw Aung San Suu Kyi was released from house arrest and I returned to her home I still listened to those songs.

Listening to these two favourite songs was my own undoing. Near the end of December 1994, I was supervising the construction of a building in Tamwe township. On December 28, 1994, at about 11pm, authorities came and searched my place for the music tapes. They seized

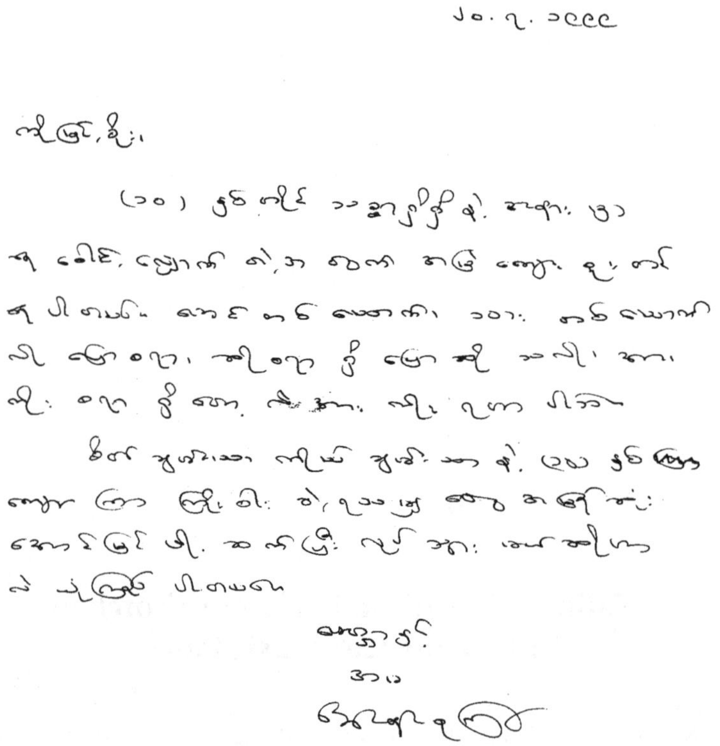

128

[Handwritten letter in Burmese script]

၂၀ . ၇ . ၁၉၉၉

[Handwritten Burmese text]

[Several lines of handwritten Burmese text]

Daw Aung San Suu Kyi's letter to the author on 20 July 1999.

all the tapes they could find and took me to the Tamwe police station. During interrogation, they asked me how the music tapes came into my possession. Although I told them the truth, they did not believe me and I was detained. When they heard of my plight, two of my friends, Ko Maw and Ko Aung, came to visit me in the morning. At about 10am I was taken to the courthouse, where the judge sentenced me to Insein Prison. I spent three days and three nights in prison and passed New Year's Day inside. On Monday morning I was released by the judge's order.

20-7-1999

Ko Myint Soe,

Thank you very much for taking care me closely and loyally for (10) years time. I feel like you are a brother or a son whom I can rely on.

I believe that you will continue to strive for success after 10 years long struggle.

with metta,

Ama

Aung San Suu Kyi

What makes me happy is hearing "National Spirit", sung by Khin Nyunt Yee, at 9am on schooldays at a primary school near the Kokkine traffic lights.

Patriotism, national spirit and a national leader are three important requirements of every country. They are the signs of nationalism.

– Open News (Vol. 4, No. 42, September 2011)

Women who came forward

"**W**omen Come Forward": this song was composed by Than Thar Win, the daughter of veteran singer Nwe Yin Win. (I used to be a fan of Joyce, Than Thar Win's mother, and Mary Conway, mother of J-me and Nu Nu Zaw living at Suniram Park, who sang the song "Jasmine Bloom-time Dear (Maung)".)

"Women Come Forward" has been sung by many modern female singers such as Chaw Su Khin, Kabyar Bwe Hmu, Me Me Khe, Than Thar Win, Shin Phone, Khin Phone, Nge Nge, Sandy Myint Lwin and Ni Ni Khin Zaw. Many female singers brought their talents to the fore with this song, including Tun Eindra Bo, Chit Thu Wai, Kyi Phyu Shin, Ei Ei Khaing, She and actresses from Thee-Lay-Thee. This group was reinforced by Soe Nandar Tun, Rebecca Win, Tin Zar Maw, Htike Htike, Sone Thin Pah, Yadanar Maing, Irene Zin Mar Myint, Khin Myat Mon and May Khalar.

During the time of our Lord Buddha, there were famous women such as Mae Daw Mar Yar, stepmother Gaw Ta Mi, Yathaw Dayar and Visakha.

Abhi Yar Zar of Tagaung started our Myanmar history not only with men but with women also. Queen Pan Htwar of the Tha Yar Khittra dynasty, Queen Saw Mon Hla and Phwar Saw of the Bagan dynasty, Queen Shin Saw Pu of the Hantharwaddy dynasty and Queen Mae Nu and Su Phyar Latt of the Kone Baung dynasty are some very famous women from our history.

Ma Daw Ohn, writer Daw Sann, Ludu Daw Amar, Daw Khin Myo Chit, Thakhin Ma Daw Sae and Thakhin Ma Daw Thein Tin were famous during the colonial era.

From the parliamentary democracy era to today, the one and the only female ambassador was Daw Khin Kyi, Daw Aung San Suu Kyi's mother.

Under the one-party dictatorial system, many exemplary women distinguished themselves in politics, such as Daw May May Aung from Yangon, Daw Aye Myint from Bago, Daw Kyi Kyi Sein from Rakhine State and Daw Kyu Kyu Marr from Shan State.

Over 20 years ago a figure said there will be no woman politician in an administrative role in Myanmar, but not long after he was the one talking happily with Pathein-born Chan Pauloo, Sheik Hassina, Khalidar Zia, Mega Waddy Sukarno and Quorazan Aquino.

In Myanmar politics women have often worked alongside men. Some people wanted the women's roles to be kept low-profile. From 1962 until May 1966, there was no such day as "Myanmar Women's Day". This day only came into existence after some people from women's organisation from a precursor to ASEAN came secretly to Myanmar.

There have been many women activists detained by the government. Hundreds of women were detained during the 1974 U Thant riots, including Mai Po Po Din (aka Ma Hla Myaing) at the Hmaing Centennial and Kathy Kyi Win, Baby Kyi Win and Nay Ye Ba Swe at the Shwedagon Pagoda strike camp who published in the *Daily Mirror* and *Myanmar Alin* daily newspapers.

Women's participation in the political movement became significant in the 1988 uprisings, when Daw Aung San Suu Kyi became a prominent figure in Myanmar politics. With the introduction of the multi-party system women became active in politics. Daw Suu became the most outstanding person in the political arena.

The list of the women detained by the government after the 1988 uprising and during the activities of June, July and August 1989 included: Dr Toe Toe Tin, Dr Khin Aye Cho, Daw Pyone Pyone Tin and Daw Saw Myat Mar on the morning of July 19, 1989; Shwee (now hluttaw representative from Nay Pyi Taw) in the afternoon; and Daw Aung San Suu Kyi, Ma Theingi, advocate Daw Myint Myint Khin, Daw Kyi Kyi and daughter Ma Done, War War Cho (Insein), Ma Kyu Kyu Than and Kyi Kyi Soe from Kachin State on July 20, 1989. There are others as well I cannot remember.

Women arrested by the government in 1990 included Daw San San (Seik Kan), Daw San San Win (Ahlone) and Daw Khin San Hlaing (Wet Let township). Arrests in 1991 included Khin Moe Aye, Aye Aye Moe, Mar Mar Oo, Moe Kalyar Oo and Hnin Hnin Phway. In 1994, it was Aye Aye Moe, Moe Kalyar Oo and Cho New Oo at U Nu's funeral. In 1996, it was Nilar Thein, Me Me, Ma Po Gyi, Lay Lay Mon, Yi Yi Aung, Ei Shwe Sin Nyunt and Yi Yi. In 1998, it was Khin Moe Aye, and in 2007 Nilar Thein, Me Me, Shwee, Khin Moe Aye, Lay Lay Mon, Nimo Hlaing, Su Su Nway and Daw Win Mya Mya (Mandalay).

Women who participated in NLD Youth in 1989 included Thin Thin Aung (*Mizzima News*), Khin Thandar, Shwee, War War Cho, Myintzu, Ma Htay, Moe Moe, Ma Po Gyi, Sabae Oo, Phyu Phyu (Hlegu), Ni Ni Wai and Kalyar (Tamwe), as well as Khin Moe Moe and Ma Po Gyi from 1990 to 1992, and Ma Po Gyi, Ni Ni Wai, San San Win (Bahan), Yi Yi Mya, Yi Yi Aung, Yin Yin Mya and Ei Shwe Sin Nyunt in 1995-1996.

Other women who came forward were Dr May Win Myint, Daw San San, Daw May Hnin Kyi, Daw San San Win (Ahlone), Nan Khin Htwe Myint, Daw Hla Hla Moe, Daw Win Mya Mya, Daw Khin Moe Moe (Taunggyi), Daw Than Htay, Daw Lei Lei, Daw Myint Myint Sein, Daw Khin Khin Win, Daw Tin Tin Win, Daw San San Aung (Shwe Kyay Si), Daw Aye Aye Mar, Mummy Mya (Kyauktada), Daw Khin San Hlaing and Daw Sandar Min.

My message is that all women can come forward and you can do it too.

If you look out at the world you will find many outstanding women politicians who have filled the top posts of their respective countries. There has been: Margaret Thatcher, Britain's first woman prime minister; Madeleine Albright, America's first woman secretary of state; Condoleeza Rice, America's second woman secretary of state; and Hillary Clinton, America's third woman secretary of state, who in four years visited 122 countries and slept 400 nights on a plane. Then there is Susan Rice, the US ambassador to the UN.

Regardless of the difference in gender, these women seem to have served better than men in these high positions where character, integrity and performance are concerned.

May I introduce some of the "hands that rock the cradle" who are influencing world affairs? Just look at: Angela Merkel, German chancellor; Julia Gillard, prime minister of Australia; Sheikh Hasina, prime minister of Bangladesh; Yinluck Shinawatra, prime minister of Thailand; Dilma Rousseff, president of Brazil; Christina Fernandez, president of Argentina; and Laura Chinchila, president of Costa Rica. Ellen Johnson Sirleaf is the president of Liberia and was the 2011 recipient of the Nobel Peace Prize, one of three women who were recipients.

These facts show that women who come up front are not wrong. So keep on moving forward.

– Open News (Vol. 4, No. 42, August 2012)

A boy who called Daw Aung San Suu Kyi "Mother"

I will write about a boy whom I met 13 or 14 years ago. He deserves to be mentioned in this book.

Many visitors came and went at Daw Aung San Suu Kyi's house at that time. Once there were some visitors who stayed for a long time. Many visitors meant more work for us. My duty was going to market and cooking and serving dishes at the house. Daw Aung San Suu Kyi assigned a boy to assist me. He was reliable and trustworthy. His only weakness was his disability. When he walked he swayed, with one foot dragging. Although he spoke audibly, it was with a trembling voice, but he was always willing to work. He was not an opportunist. One could say he had a slave mentality. No one knew his real name. Although he was Myanmar, we called him by the nickname of "Arafat". Depending on our age we addressed Daw Aung Suu Kyi as Ama (sister), but he called her *Amae* (mother). Staying at the beck and call of Daw Aung San Suu Kyi, I had to be wary and vigilant, but as for Arafat, I trusted him completely.

Arafat lived near the Tamwe roundabout. Because of his disability, busmen refused to take him on their buses and he had to walk to reach Daw Aung San Suu Kyi's home. He did all kinds of house chores. Working in a sitting position was most suitable for him. At 6pm it was time for him to leave for his home. He used to pay homage to *Ama* upstairs everyday when he arrived to the front of the house.

Once, someone asked him going to the General Post Office as an errand. On his return I asked Arafat where he had been and he replied that he had come back from the General Post Office. This building is situated on Strand Road and Arafat had had to walk from Kokkine. One can imagine how far he had to walk. It showed Arafat never shirked from work.

Eight days after the photo of Arafat and Daw Aung San Suu Kyi was taken, Arafat died from injuries sustained after falling down the

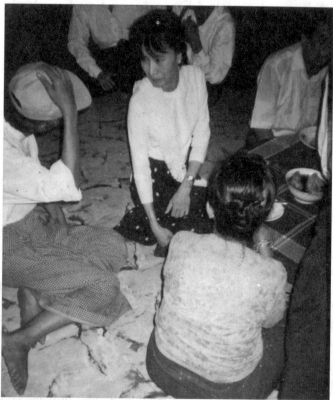

Arafat (a) Hla Myo Thwin meets Daw Aung San Suu Kyi for the Last time on June 15, 2002.

Daw Aung San Suu Kyi with her close comrades after release from house arrest in 1995.

staircase of the building where he lived. His flat was situated on the eighth floor. He was used to tumbling but on that fateful day his head struck the brick steps. I did not know about his death until I read about it in the obituary section of a newspaper: Hla Myo Thwin, aka Arafat. Although I knew only him, with the aid of my friends I went to his home and conveyed my condolences to his family.

(Salute to Brother Arafat)

People who share a destiny with the native of Natmauk

National leader of *Myanmar-Naing-Ngan*, Father of the Tatmadaw, Commander-in-Chief and War Minister – those were the many distinguished ranks of Bogyoke Aung San. Recently, those making a movie about the life of this great man finally chose the cast, including two men to portray Bogyoke and two women for the role of Daw Khin Kyi.

The film will be completed in time for the birthday centenary of Bogyoke Aung San which falls on February 13, 2015, which is two years away. The film will be made with the advice and assistance of domestic and foreign experts.

Where Bogyoke Aung San was concerned, there has always been a fire in the minds of the people. My thinking was that when the opportunity arose they would talk openly about him. As my thinking has turned out right, I am very happy.

I do not make friends with people who speak ill of Bogyoke and his family. I am friendly to people who speak well of them. When they arrested me it was at Bogyoke Aung San's family home. Daw Aung San Suu Kyi was put under house arrest on July 20, 1989, and after nearly six years she was freed on July 10, 1995. I was imprisoned for five years and on my release I went back to Daw Aung San Suu Kyi.

Our team consisted of 30 people. Among those returning to Ama's service were Ko Aung Kyaw Oo, Ko Maw Min Lwin, Ko Aung Gyi Lwin and me. I was given the duty of chef, which was appropriate because I like to cook. When it comes to food, Daw Aung San Suu Kyi is not fussy, but she eats moderately, and puts emphasis on healthy foods, with less oil and salt and no monosodium-glutamate (MSG). Belly of short-headed catfish curry is part of her diet which includes fish oil (Omega-3). She always has a vegetable dish at each of her meals. When people say Daw Aung San Suu Kyi has a thin, body-conscious figure, I would advise them to follow Daw Aung San Suu Kyi's eating habits. They will be healthy without going to the gym or exercising.

I never used to listen to what people said to me for my own good, especially when it related to my bad eating habits. I have changed now. I eat what is good for my health, with less salt and more fish belly curry. I now follow Daw Aung San Suu Kyi's eating habits.

Now, let me bring this back again to the subject of the plan to make a film depicting Bogyoke Aung San's life. The production of this film depends on one man, and that person is Kadongyi (bald head), aka Ko Zarganar. I do not know when he started planning this movie. He said that if he did not get permission to film here, he would do it abroad. I think we first met in 2006 at the home of my friend U Myint Thein who was the hluttaw representative from Mon State in 1990 and who was also a friend of Daw Aung San Suu Kyi's. *Ama* always gave me some of a pizza-like snack whenever she made it. I didn't used to eat them and brought them instead to U Myint Thein, whose health by then had deteriorated (U Myint Thein passed away not long ago). One day Ko Zarganar was there at U Myint Thein's house and when I learned that he was very respectful of Bogyoke, gave him half of the snack. When U Myint Thein told him that this was no ordinary pizza but had been personally made by Daw Aung San Suu Kyi, he was surprised. Kadongyi remembered this incident and on his return from prison at Myitkyina, when people asked what he wanted most, he replied that he wanted to eat Daw Aung San Suu Kyi's pizza. Nobody else would have known the meaning of what he said at that time. Only U Myint Thein and I knew. I smiled when I read about it in a journal. Even *Ama* did not know, because she gave the snack only to me and I did not tell her who else I was giving it to. Kadongyi, like me, is devoted to Daw Aung San Suu Kyi.

Another person who deserves respect is Ko Maung. When Kadongyi's parents passed away, on each occasion Daw Aung San Suu Kyi asked me to give funeral wreaths. I personally wrote the condolences on the funeral wreaths and took them to the funeral homes. As Kadongyi was in prison and therefore absent, Ko Maung filled his place and received the funeral wreaths from me. Ko Maung was a caring and responsible person. He kept the funeral wreath until the flowers became wilted. Then he wrote an article asking for the true owner of the funeral wreaths to come and fetch them. I do not know whether Kadongyi knew about this. I already knew all about it when I read the article.

When they met, Kadongyi would have told Daw Aung San Suu Kyi about the movie. Their thinking would have been the same. Before long there was news in the media of the planned movie. I was very happy. "If U Myint Thein were alive, how happy he would be," I thought.

Kadone Gyi (Zagana) and Ko Maung (Kyaw Thu) at the alms offering to the monks at Bronze Pagoda during the saffron Revolution, September 2007.

After Kadongyi and Aung San Suu Kyi met, committees were formed, meetings took place and the opening of offices resulted. It was a wonderful occurrence. Would-be actors were interviewed and preliminary selections were made. During that time – I think it was in mid-April – in front of No. 97B Shwegondine Road I saw a girl dressed in the sort of attire which our mothers wore. This girl resembled Daw Khin Kyi. I befriended the man who accompanied her and persuaded her to apply for the role of Daw Khin Kyi. The man told me that he had undergone training as a film director and that the girl was also interested. I directed them to the office of the Bogyoke Aung San film organising committee. When I asked her about herself, she said her age was 29 years, she was from Pathein, she worked as a teacher and she was temporarily staying at U Po Kya Road, Kandawgalay. I jotted it all down.

At that time Kadongyi was abroad. I told Ko Aung Tun, who was my friend, that Ma Zar Chi Lin who resembled Daw Khin Kyi would be coming to him. The next time I met Ko Aung Tun, he told me that Ma Zar Chi Lin had come to apply for the role of Daw Khin Kyi and that he thought the girl was suitable for the role.

On July 20, 2012, when I saw Daw Aung San Suu Kyi interviewing the applicant and the committee members chuckling, I thought that she would be chosen, and indeed, when an announcement was made in the newspaper on July 25, 2012, her name was in the number one spot. One could say this was the result of deeds done in past lives.

– The Myanmar Times (Vol. 30, No. 581, 2012)

To be recorded in history
(part I)

Times are changing so fast as days go by. I am pleased with these unexpected changes, some of which are things I only dreamed of before.

I sincerely respect and honour the morality and way of thinking of the reformers, including President U Thein Sein, Executive House Speaker Thura U Shwe Mann, peace negotiator U Soe Thein and U Aung Min.

On the other hand, I also hear so many stories about people who want to reverse the wheel of history. They talk to the people here and there and let the world know about them. As the proverb says, speaking too much show one's character and philosophy follows the words. Of course, contradictions will always arise somewhere, but I am a democrat and will always support and honour developments and reforms.

I believe in the will and sincerity of those reformists who acknowledge the 1988 democratic uprising and the role of *Ama* and her father. There might be some people who want to turn back history. President U Thein Sein has clearly stated that he will leave those people behind. This is the only path to be taken and we will have to drop those who are not on pace with modern Myanmar.

A weekend speech made by Daw Aung San Suu Kyi in 1995. (Left to Right) U Tin Oo, Daw Aung San Suu Kyi and U Kyi Maung.

We can no longer look at our own country like someone seeing the moon through a bamboo pipe. We have to open our eyes to see the international community also. The world is becoming like a village. Laptops are replacing slate writing tablets. It is nonsense to talk about turning back history while sitting in front of a laptop.

It is necessary to avoid tricky ways and lies when dealing with the people. Don't push people to believe only what you say. I would like to quote the words of Dr Aung Tun Thet: "It is good to have disagreement in ideas and it is not dangerous to have differences. We can look at a matter from different angles as long as we have many different opinions. Then we can see the problems more clearly."

Now is the time for change and reform. As we enter a new era, I have an episode from the past in my memory. A day of trouble came to me and *Ama* at the same time. I believe that we both have the same karma and must be suffering together for past misdeeds.

I have sent food and necessary things to *Ama* daily without taking a holiday for more than 20 years: no holiday in weeks, in months, in years. I have done my duty regularly to allow *Ama* to have fresh food every day. *Ama* is a woman of discipline and I have always carried out the tasks as she said. She always has a timetable and is systematic in everything.

In contrary, I have no discipline and I live my life as I like. I don't even put on a watch and I don't care about the time either. I hate watches, even platinum-coated Rolexs with diamonds. I don't want that kind of watch. That is why *Ama* is patient when she asks me to do things for her. Anyway, I have never been absent from my duty for Ama.

Ama also is very dutiful. Every time I send her food, she always hosts me with tea, coffee and snacks. I refuse to have those as I can have them outside, but she always insists on my having some or tells me to take them away and give them away to someone. I always consider things from her side and don't want to bother her. Sometimes I have to wait for her the whole day and I am given cold drinks and snacks. She always gives me some snacks every evening before I go home. She also sends the fruit which we pick in the compound to her friends and dear ones. Mangoes, *mayan (bouea burmanica), thitto (santol)* and

Daw Aung San Suu Kyi; giving speech after release from house-arrest on July 10, 1995.

cabbage are the things I have to send. My quota is always included. I take my quota and I always give away the rest to other people. People with the same karma will meet one other, I believe. Ko Kyaw Thu and Ma Shwe Zee Kwet also had mangoes from Ama's compound, and *mayan* were sent to the 88 Generation.

When my house was blown away by Cyclone Nargis I had to live somewhere else. When *Ama* found out she gave me some shirts, longyis, towels, toothpaste, a toothbrush and soaps. I refused to take them but *Ama* forced me to accept them. I always keep Ama's presents in recollection of her and I value them highly, but I have to use up toothpaste and soap before they go bad.

I remember one amusing thing to mention. I always throw away the bags of trash from Ama's house at a dump site near Kokkine. When my friends, including Ko Kyaw and his son, saw me with the trash bags, they used to tease me, saying, "The bottle buyer is coming." *Ama* is very systematic and puts the kitchen garbage in one bag, household trash in one bag and her own trash in a separate bag. I never bring Ama's trash bag as I don't want other people to see it. Boxes and bottles are included in the trash and they so call me "bottle buyer".

She used to wash the plastic bags and dry them in sun, then she would fold the dried plastic bags in the shape of a triangle and give them to me, saying that I should give them to other people to reuse them. I always take them and give them to Ko Kyaw's shop.

Ama never wastes time and she is always busy with one thing or another. She always does things by herself. Only when she cannot do it does she ask others to repair or buy something for her.

If she wants to repair something she first packs the item systematically with paper or clothes around it before giving it to me. I have to memorise the packing pattern to be able to repack it like she does when I return it. If it is not thoroughly packed she will not like it and may scold me. When she orders wooden bookcases and small cupboards, she makes a detailed drawing and marks inches or centimetres exactly. If the finished product is not correct in its dimensions she will reorder it in the correct size. Ama's relative Ko Aung Kyaw Oo is the one who deals with that kind of job and he sometimes has to do things several times in accordance with her wishes. Ko Aung Kyaw Oo is very busy

Press-briefing on July 11, 1995 after release from house-arrest on July 10, 1995.

and sometimes he gives instruction to his followers to carry out Ama's orders. So many accidents happened, like the paper with the drawing would get lost or the incorrect dimensions would be made, that I used to make four or five copies of her drawings to avoid her disappointment.

Especially when repairing watches and radios, I have to find friendly and fast repair shops. I have to wait and watch the repairing until it is done. I have to take care to carry out the tasks assigned by Ama, even though it is sometimes dangerous.

The hundredth anniversary of Daw Khin Kyi's birth was in 2012. In one article I read about Daw Khin Kyi I found the wrong year of birth was given (1916) and her father's name was also wrong (U Bo Chin, instead of U Pho Hnyin). I mention this as I want the next generation to know the correct history because Bogyoke Aung San and Daw Khin Kyi are great people in Myanmar.

One book advertisement said: "This book is about Daw Aung San Suu Kyi. You will be out of date if you do not read it. Hurry to buy it at bookshops or from agents."

One of Ama's bodyguards showed me an article from *Mainichi Daily News* which took some paragraphs from *Freedom from Fear* which had been written by Ama's Japanese associate. It was only a copy. I would like to urge those making these books to thoroughly research the historical record before writing.

— *The Myanmar Times (Vol. 30, No. 584, August 31, 2012)*

To be recorded in history
(part II)
Ama vs Article 10(b)

The first Myanmar constitution was promulgated in 1947. The second constitution was adopted in 1974. Included in the 1974 Constitution was Article 10, the law safeguarding the state from subversive elements. If someone was charged under 10(a), he or she could be detained up to three years in prison with remand every six months (or released at any time). If charged under 10(b), a person could be put under house arrest for three years.

People did not pay attention to that law until 1989, but most people were aware of a different article, Article 5. I had known about it since childhood. Article 5 was the one that U Kyaw Nyein and Bo Khin Maung Galay were charged under in the 1950 Emergency Act. The parliamentary democracy government used Article 5 to detain anyone. That article was very well known since then. The Revolutionary Council also used this law after 1962.

Article 5(j), similar to Article 5 from 1947, was included in the 1974 Constitution. Most people did not know about it then. Article 5(j) might have been what was used to charge the demonstrators who participated in the 1974 workers' strike, the 1974 U Thant uprising, the 1975 workers' strike and the centennial of Thakhin Ko Daw Hmine in

1976. Article 5(j) became very familiar to the public after 1988. Someone could be charged under Article 5(j) and detained for a maximum of 45 days. If the government wanted to detain that person longer, that person could be charged under Article 10(a) and the sentence could be extended to three years in prison, as has been practised since 1989. Article 5(j) and the articles for high treason (122 and 124) were very often invoked in previous eras.

Starting from early 1989, the notorious Insein Prison was flooded with those charged under

Article 5(j) and Article 10(a). The first batch included Ko Myat San and Ko Paw Oo. The second batch, in June, included U Win Tin, Ko Soe Thein and Thura U Ngwe Hlaing, Shwee (hluttaw representative Daw Sandar Minn), Dr Toe Toe Tin, Ma Saw Myat Mar, Daw Pyone Pyone Tin, Dr Khin Aye Cho, Daw Aung San Suu Kyi, Daw Kyi Kyi and her daughter Ma Doe and son-in-law Ko Moe Win, as well as other political activists listed in the Red Book and Green Book published by the then-government. All charged under Article 5(j) had their sentences extended under Article 10(a).

Starting from that time we were all becoming familiar with articles 5(j) and 10(a). Democracy and Peace Party Executive members were also put under house arrest with Article

10(b), as I later found out after my release from Insein Jail. Articles 5(j), 10(a) and 10(b) were the most common political charges during 1989 and 1990. The articles prescribed in 1974 law were officially implemented at that time.

Someone charged under a political article should be called a "political prisoner". It was very awkward to call them "prisoners of conscience", like seeing a vulture and calling it a golden hamsa as in the story. That might be the real reason to put our country on the list of Least Developed Countries (LDCs).

Ama had a war of words with the authorities about Martyrs' Day on July 19, 1989. This was the starting point of a new phase in history, you could say. At 4am *Ama* decided not to march to Martyrs' Mausoleum. The decision had to be made public through the township NLD members.

While spreading the news of Ama's decision, Dr Toe Toe Tin, Ma Saw Myat Mar, Daw Pyone Pyone Tin and Dr Khin Aye Cho were the first to be arrested, in a car in South Okkalapa. People who did not know the decision were crowded near Shwedagon Pagoda. The group led by Shwee was confronted by security forces on Ko Min Ko Chin Road and near the ice shop bus stop. Other people were arrested there also in a second batch.

July 20, 1989, was a historic date for Ama and Article 10(b). University Avenue was quiet in the early morning in front of Ama's residence and NLD headquarters. Only some residents, our colleagues and the office staff were moving around. There were also some visitors coming in and making enquiries about yesterday's events.

About 9am, there were no cars passing by. Some returned home and some stayed to watch the situation. At about 10am, security forces blocked the whole street and took positions in all directions around the compound. Nobody was allowed to trespass on the compound. They blocked the connections between the compound and the headquarters. People tried to send in lunch (rice and curry) to headquarters through the primary school compound but later on this route was cut off too. The security forces gave us a hand in buying tea, coffee, snacks, betel-quid and cigarettes via their assistants, though, and we were grateful to them for their help.

Some authorities came to the gate at about 5pm with a letter requesting to see Ama. As we opened the gate the security forces moved in left and right and quietly occupied the whole compound. It was like a war column, with some of them carrying backpack communication devices. Everyone in the compound except Ama's relatives who were gathered in the assembly tent were surrounded by the security forces.

Nobody was allowed to enter Ama's residence then. Names were taken down of the people in the tent. We were thirsty at that time as we were running out of drinking water there. We were not allowed to take water from outside either.

At about 8pm, two people were brought into the building which was still under construction. Later we learned that Bagyi Moe (Maung Moe Thu) and U Soe Thein (Maung Wun Tha) were there. We saw their details being taken down.

At 9pm, the people in the tent were summoned in rows of two and made to sit on the road in front of Ama's house. *Ama* appeared on the porch and gave us water and said farewell to us. Then we walked to the gate where TE-11 Hino military trucks were stopped. We climbed up into the trucks two at a time while they watched us with flashlight beams and videotaped our movement.

Two truckloads of people were covered with canvas. The trucks started to move, turning right to University Avenue and then to Insein Road at the Hledan juncture. After a half-hour drive the truck started to rumble like it was driving on a dirt road. A few minutes later the truck driver was ordered to reverse and I heard the sound of us hitting something. After that the truck moved forward a little bit and the engine was stopped.

When they opened the canvas I could see the red gate of Insein Prison, also called "the gate of the university", "*Narathein*", "Big School", "Insein Retreat" and "Narani Prison". I had to exclaim, "*Buddha!*"

Ma Theingi was escorted by female police and U Moe Thu and U Soe Thein were escorted away together. Ko Htein (U Win Htein), the Meiktila hluttaw representative, was taken away, as was Ohn Kyaw Myint. The rest of us – Ko Myint Swe (Tin Swe Moe), myself and others – were searched by the police. They recorded our money, watches, pens and rings individually.

Then we were brought to a one-storey building along the dirt road. We were told to go into the fourth room which was about 100 feet by 50 feet. (The building is no longer the same as it was then.) The room was large enough for us and we learned that about 800 people could be put in a room of this size.

A moment later, prison officials brought dinner for us: a plate of rice and a spoonful each of black-coloured shrimp paste. No one could eat. I looked around. The hall had big windows fenced with iron bars. The hall was illuminated with many fluorescent lights and search lights were aimed at our room from outside. Later some friendly prison officials told us that they had not slept the night we were brought in. They had been briefed that we were commandos of Daw Suu. That was why they had aimed their guns at us when we were walking along the lane, and why they pointed search lights at our room the whole night.

Actually, we were peaceful people, as they later found out. It was an awkward briefing, they said.

There were over 30 people in the hall, including Ko Tin Swe Moe, his group of Ama's followers and the employees of a tea shop by the compound gate owned by Ama's cousin Ko Soe (Ko Soe Aung). We saw some bamboo mats and put some down for beds, but we could not sleep as we had no pillows and blankets. Everyone was dazed: we had never been to jail and we could not speak to each other for worrying.

I was thinking about Ama. She had been put under house arrest. How would it be? There might be some guards at least. Perhaps Ma Sein and Maria could stay together with Ama, I thought. What about the people from NLD headquarters? How about the NLD youth from Yangon Division? How about Ba Soe and Ba Win? Is everything okay with Amay Chaw? What is the situation outside? So many things were in my thoughts. I fell asleep late, in the middle of the night.

Next morning, a prison official introduced a man named Ko Myint Kyaw Oo and said that he would be our leader. They said that Ko Myint Kyaw Oo was a veteran and was imprisoned for attacking Dala Police Station during the 1988 uprising. He used to stay at the office the whole day and came to our hall late in the evening.

The toilet consisted of two big glazed earthen pots, one for urination and one for defecation. As there was no partition we fixed up some bamboo mats in one corner. When we went to the toilet we had to use bamboo sticks because water was not provided for cleaning ourselves. After a while the first bamboo mat of six feet by five feet was gone.

We could hear voices from the next room. According to our leader, they were from the people who had been captured on July 19. One prison policeman came. He opened the door and two men in white shirts carried in a tub behind him. They had come to collect urine and excrement. When we talked to those people they didn't respond and did not even look at our faces. Later we found out that no one was to speak with us and if they did and were found out, they would be given severe punishments.

Drinking water was supplied daily in small pots. Our hall leader always gave me food and things to be kept for him. He told me that betel-quid and cheroots could be shared with others. Some smokers were happy with the cheroots and the betel-quid would do for me.

At about 10am aluminum plates were filled with rice and bean curry together with a spoonful of the black shrimp paste. We had no experience with prison lunches of this kind and we didn't know how to eat it, but we swallowed the rice and bean curry to fill our empty stomachs. I didn't like shrimp paste and I never took it, but fried chillies went well with the bean curry.

The evening meal of steamed vegetables, rice and shrimp paste was given at 4pm. Spiny amaranth and other vegetables (sometimes even grass) were included in the meal. They called it tar ta paw soup. The tender spiny amaranth was tasty to me.

People were taken in groups to the first room of the building in the afternoon. Biographies and photos were taken by the authorities. When we were walking to the room, the windows of other rooms were blocked with bamboo mats so we would not be seen by other prisoners.

After that we were allowed to bathe at the twenty-foot-long brick water-tank. We were told by the prison guards not to talk with other prisoners from nearby buildings. One guard stood at one end and gave orders to take one cup of water at a time. We used aluminum plates to cup the water. Some people did not wait for the order and continued bathing but the guard did not say anything to us. It was not convenient to take baths without soap.

The hall closed at 6pm and the people working in our hall went to their rooms. The prison guards on duty changed also. Those guards never spoke with us as they had been given instructions not to talk by their superiors.

Before the hall closed our leader, Ko Myint Kyaw Oo, came back. He was the only one who spoke with us and he told us that we were being charged under 5(j)/(NYA). Prison people used the term "Gaw Night" to describe this charge ("Gaw" means "5" in Chinese and "NYA" means "night" in English). We would be charged or could be released after 45 days, he said. At first we thought he meant only five nights in prison but it was Article 5(j) he was talking about, as we found out later.

After three days in prison I was called by name at about midnight and prison guards brought me out of the room. They put a white cover on my head and walked along holding my arm. I had to turn left, turn right and turn around with my head down on the way to a room. Actually the path was straight, but they used psychology to make sure I would not remember the way. I had to stand and wait and when the official arrived they let me sit down and started the interrogation. Sometimes there were three or four officials questioning me. They shined a torch-light on me so I could not see them.

Employees from Ko Soe's tea shop were released on July 27 and July 28. Bagyi Pyay, who cooked for the NLD youth, and Hilux pickup driver Ko Hla Tun were released on July 31. The remaining people were Ama's acquaintances.

Those who were arrested in the compound on July 22 and remained in Insein Prison were: U Moe Thu (Bagyi Moe), U Soe Thein (Maung Wun Tha), Ma Thein Gi (Gi), Ko Htein (Meiktila hluttaw representative), Ko Myint Swe (Tin Swe Moe), Ko Maw (now in Japan), Ko Aung (now in USA), Ko Aung Kyaw Oo, Ko Khin Maung Kyaw (Atar), Ko Htein Lin Aung, Ko Myo Thein, Ko Htin Kyaw (now in Japan), Ko Kyaw Thura Ko Ko, Ko Zaw Min Oo aka Bunny (now in Ama's compound), Pyaw Bwe Maung Soe, Ko Moe Myat Thu (elder brother of DVB writer Ma Thida), Ko Paw Lwin Oo (La Bamba), Ko Aung Kyaw Moe (son of Kyauk BeLa), Sonny Kalyar, Ko Ko Gyi (now in Australia), Ko Myo Kywe (Ko Myo, deceased), Ko Moe Kyaw Thu (Jim Brown), Ko Mg Mg Oo (now in Ama's compound), Ko Thein Lwin (Thar Kayta), Ko Win Myint Oo, Ko Sann Win (released in December), Ko Kyaw Swar (artist, released), Ko Kyi Win (Rakhine) and Ko Myint Soe.

Major Than Tun (ex-Brigadier General, now in Khan-Tee prison), prison department director General Colonel Zaw Min, prison administrator Major Ohn Pe and prison doctor Dr Tun Lwin came and talked to us on August 1. They told us to tell them of our needs and inconveniences as well as our health problems. We requested to see our family members and to receive extra clothes, a more convenient toilet, the ability to read books and newspapers and medical checkups.

Major Than Tun explained to us that we could not make contact with outside or meet our family members at that time. Major Than Tun talked with Colonel Zaw Min and was told to arrange prison dress and blankets. Colonel Zaw Min said that prison dress could be issued only to prisoners (we were only being "detained" until Article 5(j), and were not technically considered prisoners) but Major Than Tun said he would take care of it and was ordered to issue prison dress to us.

A wooden seat and steps were added to the big clay pot and a water pot was also provided, making the toilet much better than before. Major Than Tun also gave instructions have medical checkups performed by a prison doctor and for hospital meals to be provided for us. (A hospital meal at that time included a piece of chicken in broth, a slice of fried fish and a loaf of pork, or two eggs for non-beef-eaters, each day). From the next day onward, the toilet was comfortable and it was good to have meals with meat and fish again.

Some oil merchants, rice traders and gold traders were arrested and were put in a room next to ours. One day a package of barlachaung (dried shrimp, shrimp paste, garlic, onion and chilli, all fried together) was received through our hall leader. The package had been sent by the owner of a department store who also acted as an oil merchant for Ama's people. Sometimes they also sent curries bought for us. Barlachaung was a very good match for the bean curry and we valued that barlachaung highly. Thanks very much, *Sein Gay Har*.

Meat curry was given every Thursday, with chicken, pork, fish and beef in rotation. Non-beef-eaters received two eggs.

Our group was kept separate from other prisoners. One time a prisoner aged over 70 was brought into our room. He had been sentenced for the rape of a girl of his granddaughter's age. If he was put together with other criminals there might have been some problems for that old man, but he was taken out of our room when the director general inspected us. The director general gave a harsh scolding to the prison director, saying that no one else could dwell with our group.

Major Than Tun came again on August 8, together with the director general and the prison director. We received one package each, sent by Ama. A towel, toothpaste and toothbrush, soap, sweets and biscuits were included in the package. Newspapers were given by Major Than Tun. The newspapers mentioned some news and press briefings about us, saying that 41 illegal tenants in the compound had been arrested. We sometimes had word of news sources from reliable sources or diplomatic sources. I only listen to news from reliable sources and I always had to see those sources whenever I could.

Major Than Tun asked us whether the arrangements of the prison officials were okay or not and we replied to him that they were okay thanks to him. When we asked him when we would be released, he replied that he didn't know when, and that it was the responsibility of higher authorities only.

Sweets and biscuits were kept and controlled by me. I had to distribute a quota to everybody daily. Pyawbwe Maung Soe and Moe Myat Thu (the son of the prison director and the younger brother of Miko) were humourous and they talked to me and tried to steal the biscuits, but I always caught them.

The building we were put in was No. 5 Ward. It was a two-storey building before but the upper wooden floor burnt down in 1988, so the remaining brick building was re-roofed as a one-storey building. It was painted just before we arrived and the flooring in the corridor was not done yet. Work on No. 5 Ward recommenced after our group arrived.

One day they started flooring the corridor in front of our room with cement. Kyan Khinn cement bags have three plys of packing paper and the middle layer is clean. We asked the masons to give us the packing paper to use as waste paper. We cut the paper into small pieces and kept them under our mats as paper was not allowed in prison.

One night Win Myint Oo behaved like a possessed one; he was crying or laughing and we all got shocks and dared not sleep the whole night. Some said as they went by that there was a Kayin woman-ghost. Starting the next day we started saying prayers, led by Ko Myint Kyaw Oo. We recited the Thira Thamein Pali verse daily until the 45 days of our 5(J) sentence in that hall were up. (I want to say thanks to Ko Myint Kyaw Oo as now I can recite that Pali verse even today.)

Two weeks after we arrived at No. 5 Ward, we saw Myint Aung (NLD youth) outside across from our room having lunch. He had put on a black *taikpone*. We exchanged smiles and laughter as we could not speak to each other. (I had first met him when *Ama* visited the San Chaung NLD office.) The next day we heard the news that Myint Aung escaped from Insein Prison by pretending to be a military intelligence official. (I have not seen Myint Aung since.)

We were very excited on September 4. Our 45 days under Article 5(j) were up and we did not know if we would be released or charged again under another article. After lunch we were told to pack our things and we were brought out of the room in rows of two. We walked to a compound labeled "Cells". One warder told me on the way that we had been charged under Article 10(a) and we would be detained for three years and remanded every six months, and that we would be put into cells.

When we arrived at the cell office, we were searched again and betel-quid was confiscated. The prison director told the warders that this group would be handled directly by military intelligence and all the supplied materials could not be confiscated. For a joke, we were told the apartment (the cell) was free of rental charges and that no deposit would be required.

This was the end of our time under Article 5(j) and the start of our time under Article 10(a).

We were sent to a nearby row of cells which had one iron-bar door and another wooden door which closed from the outside. We could not see the sky as the cell was totally closed. We had to stay there for a while and then we were brought to another building with dark cells. The first one was called Cell No. 6 and the one we had to stay in was Cell No. 5, which they called a death-house. There were 22 cells and one empty cell in the building. What we learned was that a prisoner sentenced to death by hanging was put in cells 1 through 22 and would be taken out from cell 22 at dawn and executed by hanging. Galon U Saw, student leader Salai Tin Maung Oo and Captain Ohn Kyaw Myint might have stayed in these cells.

Six of us – Ko Tin Swe Moe, Ko Maw, Ko Aung, Maung Maung Oo, Thein Lwin and I – were put into cell 15. We were in the death-house and the feeling came over us that we might be hanged, but when we remembered we had been charged under Article 10(a), not sentenced to death, we were a little relieved.

Cell No. 5 was very cool even in the middle of the day as there were water tanks under the building. We found it was very crowded for six of us to stay in the small room of 10 feet by 10 feet. In the past this kind of room would have been occupied by only one prisoner, but now there were more prisoners than previously. The reasons were as follows.

The government had strategically planned to hold the election in 1990. Tactically it allowed the formation of political parties with the enticement of one landline telephone and barrels of gasoline for each party. All sorts of parties sprung up, numbering more than 200 and spanning all ages, young and old, each with different experiences and exposures. Undercover parties were also included.

Ama, the daughter of Aung San, had graduated with a Political Science degree, so it should have been no surprise that she was interested in politics. During the Socialist era, government advisors and astrologers foretold that the king-to-be would emerge from a famous family at that time. The head of state himself felt agitated and asked Ama, "Suu Suu, are you not taking part in politics, or are you interested in politics?" At that time Ama replied, "I am living here and I am not taking part in politics."

On August 15, 1988, Ama and U Htway Myint wrote an open letter to the State Council suggesting the formation of an advisory committee to handle the current situation in Myanmar. At that time "The Patron" or "Bel Air Hla Myint" rushed to Ama and told her, "Suu Suu, you said in England that you will not take part in politics and now you have entered politics by writing the letter dated August 15, 1988."

Ama replied, "I was saying that I will not do any politics while I was staying there (in England) but I was not saying I will not do politics in Myanmar."

Later Ama and the secretary of the State Council talked on the phone and had some discussions in person. Ama had had an appointment for a meeting with the last president before 1988 but the appointment had been cancelled. (Ama started her political role with state-level authorities.)

Ama started making addresses at the Yangon General Hospital on August 23, 1988. On the stage together with Ama were Bagyi Thaw (Maung Thaw Ka) and Khin Thida Tun (actress). In front of the stage were Maung Thway Thit (poet), Ko Myo Nyunt (Sarpay Lawka), Ko

Myo Myint Nyein, Mahar Nandar Ko Myo Win, Wut Yee Ko Lay and Literature Union members. On August 26, 1988, *Ama* gave a historic speech at the western gateway of the Shwedagon Pagoda. Lay Lay (Actor U Tun Wai) was at her side there. *Ama* showed her father's nature on that day.

Then the smear campaign started against Ama. Posters with "wife of an Indian" written on them were posted everywhere downtown. One pickup loaded with posters was caught at midnight by local people at the corner of Anawrahta Road and Shwebontha Road. The group, including one army officer was interrogated at the Shwebontha Buddhist community hall. They were transferred to Thayet Taw monastery. The incident was reported to *Ama* and she was shown the nasty posters. *Ama* is attached to the soldiers as she grew up among them. She asked the monks to release the people.

That officer's name was very famous at that time. He was predestined to meet with *Ama* again ten years later, in September 1998, at the bridge near Kyi Su village on the way to Nyaung Done. That time the officer didn't give his real name but *Ama* remembered and used the name he had used in Thayet Taw monastery. That young officer is retired now. Those who had ill will toward *Ama* disappear each day and the daughter of Bogyoke Aung San still retains her good name.

Political parties were categorised into old political groups, pro-government groups, leftist groups, BCP (Burma Communist Party) groups and student groups. Government people infiltrated the parties and tried to destroy the unity of each party. The government accused the NLD of harbouring communists and said that the party helped the underground. Those were tactics to destroy the parties in 1989 before the election was held in 1990. Tactics to destroy the NLD started in December 1988 but after that the NLD became even more unified and stronger than before. Colonel Kyi Maung changed to Ama's side and the NLD attracted a lot of top military officers. The core of the NLD included Brigadier General Aung Shwe (ex-ambassador to many countries), Colonel U Shwe (ex-Revolutionary Council member, minister), Colonel Lun Tin (Divisional Commander, Northwestern), General Thura Tin Oo (ex-chief of staff), Colonel U Lwin (ex-deputy prime minister), Colonel Kyi Maung (Divisional Commander, Southwestern), Colonel Hla Pe (Divisional Commander, Eastern); as well as members of the Patriotic

Veterans Organisation, including Colonel Chit Khaing, Colonel Soe Thane, Colonel C Vin Kyu, Colonel Khin Maung Tun, Colonel Saw Mya Thein (father of Saw Myat Mar), Colonel Tin Ko Ko, Colonel Min Nyi, Major Ba Thaw (Maung Thaw Ka) and Captain Win Htein (hluttaw member).

Ama was warmly welcomed by the local people when she made organisational tours to the states and divisions. She was like her father Bogyoke Aung San when she made speeches for two hours straight without reading from any paper.

Ama can communicate with foreigners without interpreter or translator. She can speak many languages: English, Japanese, French, Indian and Bhutanese also. She learned like her father did and had a good education under the guidance of her mother. She became involved in politics like her father as she wants our country to be prosperous. She never used the influence of her father's name to take a share of the country's resources. She understands politics very well and she has sacrificed by giving up family affairs for the sake of her country. Like father, like daughter.

Her organising tours followed the same pattern as her father's. People gave respect and love to her. The country had been totally closed for 26 years and a ray of hope for the future had come out into the open. At that time the government changed its tactics and began to threaten Ama and prohibit her movements. One time she was told not to cross a line or she would be shot. The soldier who aimed his rifle at Ama was very angry at the time that he was not allowed to shoot. He was a hero to his group.

The government then tried a new way: to trim down the branches from the tree until it stood alone as a bare trunk. They started this strategy in March 1989 by arresting Myat San and Paw Oo. They took the "Three Colours" from Ama in June and detained U Win Tin, U Soe Thein and Thura U Ngwe Hlaing. Their target was Martyrs' Day. They tried to pull down the whole tree at that moment. Ama responded by saying, "To defy all the unfair orders is our duty." They drove a wedge between the "Patriotic Veterans" and Ama. All the BCP UGs were arrested in connection with *Dawn* magazine. Also, the OG and UG activists from all parties were arrested in July, August and September

1989. These were the main causes of the over-crowded prisons.

(The government, wanting to the people to forget Martyrs' Day and all state-level displays of respect for it, used to assign drainage cleaning, repairing roads and general fatigue duties on Martyrs' Day.)

Marches and wreath-laying at Martyrs' Mausoleum is Myanmar's historical inheritance. People will go there to lay wreaths and then will go home. It is not an armed riot. If the government suspected something, they could assign some armoured cars to patrol the streets. During the 1970 Students' Festival, they put armoured cars and fire engines near Thamada cinema. People will disperse if they are given signals or hear the bang of a gunshot in the air. (Recently there had been demonstrators holding guns and driving cars in convoy in Myawaddy who were not arrested or charged. The public was told that even monks were shot so they brought the weapons to respond in case they were shot. The peaceful demonstrators without arms were arrested, charged and put in prison. We thought that we would not be charged if we demonstrated without holding weapons.)

We heard that movie-director Maung Khet Pan (now deceased) was also in Ward 5. During bathing time we had to go one room at a time and we were told not to talk to other people from other rooms. We saw Maung Khet Pan walk in front of our cell but we dared not talk to him. One day Pan Thee (Tun Myat Oo) from Ward 4 came and greeted us.

Each night we paid homage to *Buddha* before sleeping. There was an image of Buddha drawn by previous prisoners on the wall and one sentence had been written: "I, the Buddha, am not a dullard." I smiled and considered the meaning: "Are you afraid now? Now you remember me, Buddha, and my dhamma. I, the Buddha, am not a fool."

When we slept, the room did not have enough space for six people. As I am a short person, I took a position lying across the top of the other's heads. Two iron baskets were in the corner for our toilet. We made a partition with bamboo mats.

Ten days after arriving at Ward 5, Daw Khin Kyi's relatives Aung Kyaw Oo and brothers received packages sent by their family for the first time. (Prisoners can see their family when they get a visitor pass, but we were only allowed to receive packages sent by them.) We

In front of Daw Aung San Suu Kyi's house; 5 minutes before release from house-arrest on 13 November 2010.

received packages by name every Monday and we had to check our names on a list and sign for receipt. When things went missing from the list the prison officials had to buy and give them to us. Sometimes the things that arrived did not accord with the list for all 23 people. We reported the matter to the director general and the officials had to buy and replace the missing things.

We waited for the package (they called it the "parcel") every Monday. Cooked meat, fried meat, snacks and cheroots were the things we received. My mother sent some cheroots and food for me but I did not smoke and I gave the cheroots to others. Some in our group did not receive any parcels because they had no contact with their relatives or their relatives lived far from Yangon, but we all shared the food and things together.

We stayed at No. 5 Ward less than one month. Then we were moved to No. 2 Ward and No. 3 Ward. Later we were all put into No. 3 Ward in one group, with those who were receiving and not receiving parcels together. Aung Kyaw Oo, Atar and Htein Lin Aung were in room 4 and Paw Lwin Oo, Aung Kyaw Moe, Sonny, Ko Ko Gyi and

Maung Soe stayed in room 5. K Myo, Jim Brown, Win Myint Oo and Sann Win were in room 6 and Htin Kyaw Myo Thein, Kyaw Thura, Ko Ko, Bunny and Moe Myat Thu were in room 7. Ko Maw, Ko Aung, Maung Maung Oo and Thein Lwin were in room 9. Ko Tin Swe Moe, Kyi Win and I were in room 10.

People who had arrived at No. 3 Ward earlier than us were U Ye Tun (son-in-law of Dr Ba Maw, father of Yuzar Maw Tun) in room 1, U Nyo Win (PPP) in room 2, Aba U Tun Tin (NLD, Yangon Division) in room 8, Ako Kha aka Sayar Min Thein Kha (Ko Win Zaw and Ma Mee Mee's brother) in room 13, Bagyi Thaw aka Maung Thaw Ka in room 11 and Moe Hein also in No. 3 Ward. Moe Hein and Bagyi Thaw were moved to No. 2 Ward later.

There were 14 rooms in No. 3 Ward. Room 1 was separated and rooms 2, 3, 4 and 5 were one group and rooms 6, 7, 8, 9 and 10 were another. Rooms 11 and 12 were separated from other rooms with a long wall. Rooms 13 and 14 were the same as 11 and 12. Each room had a four-foot-square iron-bar-screened window. Ventilation was good.

There were three brick water-tanks for bathing in No. 3 Ward, one near room 1, another one in front of room 6 and the other in front of room 12. Prisoners were allowed one by one to wash their faces and bathe. We saw U Ye Tun and U Nyo Win came to bathe, but we were not allowed to speak to each other. The room was opened at 7am for face-washing, and the toilet was cleaned by workers every day. At the time of morning break we had chance to talk with people from other rooms, but if the warder found out we were told not to. Another famous prisoner in Ward 3 was U Aung Tun (aka Ako Kha, aka Sayar Min Thein-Kha). U Ye Tun used to call U Aung Tun "my friend". We gave both of them nicknames: "Aung Tun Lay" (Kid Actor) and "Ye Tun Lay" (Young Ye Tun). They used to exchange stories for about an hour whenever they bathed together in front of room No. 6.

(No. 3 Ward is not the same now as it was before. They closed the windows with bricks and a long wall of fencing was put in front of the rooms.)

U Ye Tun is the son of Justice Minister U Chan Tun, who was a member of the 1947 Constitution drafting committee. He is married to Daw Ohnmar Maw, daughter of Dr Ba Maw, and has one son, Okkar

Maw Tun, and one daughter, Yuzar Maw Tun. He was imprisoned many times for political activities during the Revolutionary Council, Socialist and SLORC eras. He grew up under a parliamentary democracy government (in the AFPFL era) and he thought that politicians were only those from that AFPFL era and their relatives, but he always supported anti-dictatorship forces. That is why he was arrested in 1989 and detained in Insein Prison. Although he supported Ama as the daughter of Bogyoke Aung San, he thought that Ama had less political knowledge than he did.

As those of us in Ama's group were staying with him in No. 3 Ward, we became friendly toward each other. He used to both support and criticise Ama. Many times I had to argue with U Ye Tun whenever he criticised Ama. Later he came to know well that I practiced "Daw Suu-ism" and we were friendly after that. We always had arguments about Ama until he passed away. We had different views and philosophies but our spirits were the same as comrade prisoners.

I met U Ye Tun and family often while shopping at City Mart and he always asked me about Ama. One time I was looking for baby-ginger jam and Dutch chocolate for Ama but I could not find it there, so I had to send some other brand to Ama. I went to U Ye Tun and asked if he might have baby-ginger jam. He replied to me that there was no more jam but he told me that he would order some from Bangkok. (I smiled because he criticised Ama and also was so generous toward her.)

Actually Ama has goodwill toward everybody and the reflections come back to her as helping hands. U Ye Tun used to say that he would buy things for Ama abroad if they could not find it here; he would ask me to drop in and have a quarrel talking about Ama. Whenever he told me that Ama should cooperate with the Government and not fight with them we would argue about it.

One day he told me that he would form a political party. I asked him with whom and he said same names. I burst out laughing and he asked why. I told him that I had already known who would be with him before he told me and that's why I was laughing. Next time we met he mentioned he didn't know what to do with his people. I replied I had already told him that people with philosophies and beliefs like Ama's will serve the country and should support Ama. It is easy to put up a party signboard but the important thing is the morale of the people.

Later he went to Singapore to be treated for his disease. After about a month, on May 7, 2010, he passed away. How happy he would be if he saw Ama cooperating with the government as he told her to, and the other changes and events taking place in our country.

– The Myanmar Times (Vol. 31, No. 603, January 2013)